HOW TO RECOGNIZE AND REFINISH ANTIQUES

FOR PLEASURE AND PROFIT

HOW TO RECOGNIZE AND REFINISH ANTIQUES FOR PROFIT

JACQUELYN PEAKE

PHOTOGRAPHY BY EDGELEY W. TODD

HARPER & ROW, PUBLISHERS, New York
CAMBRIDGE, PHILADELPHIA, SAN FRANCISCO
LONDON, MEXICO CITY, SÃO PAULO, SYDNEY

Grateful acknowledgment is made for permission to reprint
figures on pages 24, 28, 31, and 34 from *Buying Antiques* by
A. W. Coysh and J. King. Copyright © 1967 by A. W. Coysh
and J. King. Reprinted by permission of Holt, Rinehart and
Winston, CBS College Publishing.

FIRST EDITION

Library of Congress Cataloging in Publication Data

Peake, Jacquelyn.
    How to recognize and refinish antiques for pleasure and
profit.

    Includes index.
    1. Antiques.   2. Antiques—Conservation and restoration.
3. Antiques—Marketing.   I. Title.
NK1125.P39   1984   745.1′028′8   83–48799
ISBN 0–06–015273–7

84 85 86 87 88 10 9 8 7 6 5 4 3 2 1

CONTENTS

$\mathcal{I}$NTRODUCTION

Not long ago I invited an elderly lady to go along with me to an antique auction in a nearby village. She was an avid collector of antiques forty or so years ago and had furnished a large home with an impressive array of good pieces. Most of them came from the homes of farm workers in her native South. The lovely furniture had been given to those people in the 1920s, when fashionable women were throwing out that "old stuff" in favor of the more modern styles then coming into vogue.

I told this gentle soul that I hoped to pick up a few pieces at the auction to refinish. Her surprised reaction was, "Why, I would have thought all the good antiques had long since been bought up!"

She soon learned the real story about today's antique market. Yes, many of the really fine antiques, those in pristine condition and of rare value, *are* in museums and elegant private homes. Every day, though, sharp-eyed men and women are buying hundreds of antique tables, chairs, china cabinets, dressers, picture frames, beds, and bookcases, and buying them at rock-bottom prices. They often pay as little as one-tenth the retail value.

They're doing it by buying antiques which are in a condition no self-respecting fine shop owner would even consider having in the place. They're buying neglected or damaged antiques, then, with love and labor, restoring them into objects of genuine beauty and value. These are the people who will sift through the junk in a secondhand store, looking for an ink-stained library table to refinish. They're the ones who sit through long auctions hoping to get a few press-back side chairs (none of which have usable seats). They're the people you find rising at dawn on Saturdays to check out a promising garage sale.

These are the adventurers of the wonderful world of antiques! And if you're the type who welcomes a challenge, who thrives on the satisfaction of creating beauty through your own effort and ingenuity—then you are one with us.

This book will explain how and why we go about this hobby/business and how you can have the same fun and potential profit that we enjoy. It's a fascinating world, as exciting as a treasure hunt, as scintillating as fine old wine, and as stimulating as a new love.

The rationale behind all this activity is actually two-pronged. First, restoring damaged pieces to good condition gives lovers of fine furniture the chance to furnish a home with quality furniture at a fraction of the cost of new pieces. Smart young adults are picking up antiques, one at a time, and restoring them to furnish their first homes or apartments. Their parents are discovering that this is a way to add distinction to a home in a manner impossible with today's mass-produced furniture. And because antiques were built at a time when fine craftsmanship was a matter of personal pride, their basic construction is often far superior to the merchandise coming from our factories today. An antique can still have excellent woods and good design regardless of the amount of dirt and wrinkled varnish veneering a table or the number of butterfly decals decorating a baby's high chair. Second, antiques are growing in value rapidly with each passing year. So, instead of becoming merely "used" the moment after purchase, as is the case with today's furniture, an antique becomes more valuable the longer it is owned. Antiques are a recognized investment and hedge against inflation.

Investment counselors today list four major areas where wary purchasers can be virtually guaranteed a reliable and large return on their money. These are: real estate, top-quality art, investment-grade diamonds—and good antiques.

The first three investments on that list normally require substantial amounts of capital. Good antiques do, too, if bought at today's prices in the better shops. However, prices on antiques in need of restoration are within the means of anyone willing to do some scouting about to find them. Then, after adding a hearty dollop of effort to achieve the transformation, it is entirely possible to multiply one's initial small investment many times over within just a few weeks.

I have a charming ash wood Victorian washstand in my living room today that is a prime example of turning a small investment into a sizable asset. It was bought at a moving sale for $15, a sad testimony to the mayhem sometimes inflicted on good furniture. The original polished finish had long ago been covered with bright red paint. Then someone evidently decided it had outlived its usefulness and relegated it to the back porch, where the once-pretty thing became a catchall for toys, tools, and trash. Subjected to generations of weather and neglect, most of the paint had worn away by the time I found it, and the wood resembled that of a long-forgotten barn. The drawer opened with dime store knobs, and the little door hung on one corroded hinge.

After a few evenings' work in the basement, though, removing the remnants of the old paint, sanding, oiling, sealing, and replacing hardware, it is now a fine example of nineteenth-century bedroom furniture. The current retail value is about $250 and going up every year.

Most people start on this hobby/business quite by accident. They inherit a family heirloom or are given a small piece in need of repairs. A little glue or varnish remover, a couple of screws or some gentle sanding later, and they've managed to put it in pretty decent shape. They're thrilled with their own success. Then, they spot another piece at a garage sale that just begs, "Take me home and fix me up!" One or two more such incidents, and you soon have a confirmed restorer, one whose confidence and expertise build with each succeeding venture.

Pretty soon, though, all those small victories begin to crowd the house. That's often when tyro antique collectors become professionals and begin "trading up" or selling. It is then that they begin to realize the profit potential in this delightful hobby.

Trading up is simply trading two or three minor pieces for one of higher value. This is the way one woman I know began her love affair with antiques. She bought two press-back chairs at a flea market, paying $4 each for them. Neither had usable seats, one lacked a hip rest, and the other's purity had been violated with mustard-colored paint. Both wobbled dangerously. In spite of all that, though, the basic designs were excellent.

She went through the renovation procedures described in various chapters of this book and ended up with two lovely side chairs. As time went on she acquired other chairs and soon had more than she could use. So she located an antique shop in town that happened to be out of good side chairs. In the window of the shop was a charming round table, just what she needed for a corner of her living room. It was priced at $175. She brought her chairs into the owner's back room and asked, "Would you trade me that table for these chairs?" The result was an immediate deal, one which benefited both the dealer and the refinisher. The dealer could easily sell each chair for $100, so her profit margin would be larger than on the sale of the table alone. And the smart trader had upgraded an original $8 purchase (plus some work and refinishing materials) into a $175 table. Everyone came out ahead on that one.

Obviously, the person who works out such a deal immediately starts thinking ahead to other such deals. From then on, the sky's the limit—whether in trading or selling—for anyone who would like to take basic restoration skills and turn them into a satisfying sideline for pleasure or extra income.

This book was written to help you do the same. With the information in the following chapters you can either furnish your home with fine antiques at affordable prices, and/or join the ranks of those happy entrepreneurs whose income is only limited by their ingenuity.

I'll show you how to avoid mistakes (based on some of mine!) and how to make your time and money most productive. Hopefully, the information will save you the heartache of irreparably damaging a nice antique simply because you didn't know the proper refinishing techniques.

Many philosophies exist on the proper method of restoring antiques. One school holds out for complete renovation, including stripping to the bare wood and taking every member apart. Another says only absolutely necessary repairs should be made and the original finish preserved whenever possible. We'll discuss both.

The book will show you the different restoration methods you can safely tackle yourself and ones which are beyond the realm of the average do-it-yourselfer. One chapter will show you where to find the best buys in antiques in need of work, and another will discuss ways to detect them under layers of grime and paint or varnish.

One chapter gives complete information on reseating chairs, and another discusses an easy way to replace missing carving on a picture or mirror frame.

The final two chapters will be for those of you who would like to capitalize on this knowledge to increase your income. They will tell you how you can best sell your restored antiques to individuals, how to place work on consignment with antique dealers, and how to start and manage your own shop if you so desire. You'll also find information on the various legal and financial aspects of selling antiques for profit.

At the end of the book you'll find a glossary of terms used in the text. This will help you understand some words and phrases which may be new to you at first.

Lifestyles are changing and not everyone who reads this book will be a homeowner with full basement, complete workshop, and unlimited space. So, most of what is described here can be completed in the average city apartment or condominium. And only a basic knowledge of tools is required.

Nostalgia is in. Americans are discovering that acquiring and using the fine furniture of generations past is one way to establish a link with our treasured heritage. The soft patina of old wood, the delicate carvings that mirror a craftsman's love of his trade, the pride of possessing a one-of-a-kind beauty—these are some of the joys of owning fine antique furniture.

You're embarking on a genuinely satisfying craft when you start restoring neglected antiques to their rightful beauty—a craft that can occupy you for a lifetime. And I'm so very happy to have you along with me on this grand adventure!

WHERE ARE THE BARGAINS IN ANTIQUES?

Half the fun of building a collection of fine antiques can be in finding them in the first place. We antique lovers are detectives at heart, and our greatest thrill is suddenly to discover a gem of a china cabinet, a delicate little Bible table, or a lovely old oval frame hidden away in some unlikely place. We quickly pay for the purchase and haul it home—as delighted with our acumen as if we had just unearthed the Rosetta stone! Like prospectors, we'll dig and sift through tons of useless junk, always confident that just around the next corner or in the next room is the very piece we need or want to fill out a collection.

This chapter will tell you just where the best places are to find those antiques at bargain prices. It is no problem, of course, to visit the fine shops and glittering shows to search for antiques. However, if you buy in one of these usual outlets, you will pay the going retail prices, and it could be several years before that initial investment increases substantially. You will be paying for someone else's ingenuity in ferreting the antiques out of their hiding places, perhaps refinishing them, and then providing a showcase while waiting for the new owner (you!) to come along. And since this book is all about helping you increase your investment in antique furniture from minimal to substantial, I'm going to share with you some *better* places to buy your treasures. This information is useful whether you're furnishing your own home for a lifetime of enjoyment or buying for resale.

Since all of these sources are "cash and carry," you'll find a station wagon or small pickup truck ideal for transporting your purchases. Some hatchbacks offer an amazing amount of interior room, but most conventional automobiles will carry only small pieces of furniture, and even then it is awkward to jockey them into a trunk or backseat. If you do own a conventional sedan or coupe, you might team up with a friend who owns a larger vehicle and go scrounging together. Offer to pay for the gas in exchange for the use of that extra cargo space.

You should take along a few "tools of the trade," too. You'll need either a yardstick or retractable tape measure. This will help you decide whether or not a charming hall tree you want to bid on at an auction will fit into your tiny foyer. A sharp knife is useful for flicking off layers of paint to see if a tabletop is actually solid oak. Soft rags and well-capped containers of soapy water and solvent come in handy for cutting through generations of grime and old wax. And you may find invaluable one or more of the better price guides to antiques available in bookstores. These give you the current retail prices of antiques so you know whether or not the asking price for that marble-topped fern stand really is a bargain.

Now, to get down to business. The four most likely places to find antiques in need of restoration and at reasonable prices are: auctions, garage sales, flea markets, and secondhand stores.

AUCTIONS

"Do I hear fifteen? Fifteen? Fifteen? Sold to the gentleman in the second row for twelve-fifty!" The auctioneer's trained voice signals another purchase by an eager buyer. And if the fellow did his homework, he probably went home with a real bargain.

Auction buffs have been acquiring bargains at these lively sales for years. Auctions are, in fact, one of the oldest recorded means of large-scale public sales. Roman conquerers auctioned off war booty in the marketplaces of their sprawling empire a full two thousand years ago. In the Middle Ages residents of London and other large English cities regularly bought at auction the luscious fruit imported from Italy and Spain by cagey merchants. Later, colonists brought the custom with them to these shores, and we still have a record of an auction being held in New Amsterdam as early as 1662.

The auction procedures we know today evolved from a variety of now-abandoned customs. It was once common practice for bidders to bid against one another as they watched a candle burn. When the candle had burned down a specified distance, usually an inch, or had burned out, the bidding was over, and the last person to enter a bid was the successful one. An hourglass was sometimes used in the same way, the winner of the merchandise being the one to shout a bid just as the last grain of sand dropped into the lower half of the glass.

Procedures may have changed, but auctions are still one of the most exciting ways to buy goods of any kind—especially antiques! Today antiques are auctioned off in four ways.

PRESTIGIOUS AUCTION HOUSES   The most glamorous auctions are those conducted by world-famous houses such as Sotheby's of London and New York. Here, fine antiques are sold for very large sums to millionaire collectors and/or dealers whose clients are the pampered darlings of the international social set. Few of us have the bank accounts to qualify as legitimate customers at one of these glittering affairs! However, these auctions, generally held in large metropolitan areas, are an important part of the novice's education. If you live in or near a big city you should occasionally attend auctions at one of these prestigious establishments. You will learn quickly how valuable fine antiques can be. You'll see knowledgeable men and women bidding thousands upon thousands of dollars for an eighteenth-century French dressing table or a massive mirror that once graced the walls of a Spanish don's mansion. Conduct a discreet survey of your own as to what those same pieces might have sold for ten years ago. Any antique dealer can give you these figures, or you can check out some old copies of antique-related magazines at the library. You'll find that the *per-*

centage increase for those antiques is greater than virtually any other commodity available, including stocks, bonds, and real estate. With that knowledge (and incentive) you can then investigate the other categories of auctions, those where *you* can begin to build your own estate by judiciously bidding for antiques.

Now, it is highly unlikely that you will find an eighteenth-century treasure lurking undetected at any of the other auctions we'll discuss here. What you will discover are mainly nineteenth-century Victorian and turn-of-the-century pieces. These will not bring the prices that flirt with five and six figures, no matter how expertly you refinish them. But you can easily double, triple, or even quadruple your original modest investment by buying carefully at these auctions.

LOCAL ESTABLISHED AUCTION HOUSES Many areas, from rural communities to large cities, have permanent auction houses which sell everything from appliances to boxes of freight-damaged merchandise. These houses may devote one evening a month to antiques. The offerings on that night may be an accumulation from many different sources. Individuals who want to sell off an entire household of antiques will commission the auction house to handle the sale. Antique dealers frequently bring in truckloads of merchandise that hasn't moved out of their shops quickly enough. Managers or owners of the auction house itself may scour the countryside searching for items to add interest to "antique night." The result is usually a good selection of both average and fine quality antique furniture.

Some permanent auction houses handle *only* antiques. Their selection is usually made up from estates and dealers' input. The quality of the antiques is often quite a bit higher than that of the auction house which only occasionally offers antiques. So are the bids! Even so, you can find excellent buys at these houses once you develop a bit of know-how. Some houses have a back room where the auctioneers put the furniture they feel is not in good enough condition to go on the floor with the beautifully refinished items. I've seen china cabinets with glass missing from the doors, bureaus with drawers that wouldn't close properly, tables with loose veneer, and chairs with frayed cane seats. Almost all were prime candidates for refinishing. Each was marked with a set price—no bidding necessary to get them. You might check to see if such a "back room" exists in the better auction houses in your area.

ESTATE AUCTIONS OR SALES You can frequently find bargains at the so-called estate auctions held at private homes. Conducted by professional auctioneers, these sales offer only the possessions of the family living in that home. Estate sales are often held in conjunction with the sale of the house and the family's move. You'll find them advertised in the classified section of the local newspaper.

Often you have to wait through the bidding on second-rate furniture, boxes of plastic kitchenware, even a doghouse or two before anything you find interesting is offered for bids. You rarely have a place to sit, either, during these auctions, so I often take along a small folding campstool.

Unlike sales in established auction houses, these sales may start at any time of the day or evening. The newspaper ad will give you the starting time of each. As with any auction you should plan to arrive at least a few minutes early to have time to view and examine the furniture to be offered.

Many estate sales will begin in the morning and go right on through the day until everything is sold. This means there's no break for lunch. In such a case, I suggest you take along something to eat and drink. Then you won't mind the waiting until the auctioneer gets to the big old walnut bed you're determined to have!

COUNTRY AUCTIONS If you live in or near a rural community you should keep up with the country or farm auctions. The advantage of these sales is that they're so far from the "big city" that casual auction-goers seldom attend. Good pieces frequently go for much less than they would at the more heavily attended city auctions. Country auctions are not always advertised in the larger newspapers. You can get announcement flyers sent to you through the mail, though, by finding out the names of rural auction companies and asking to be put on their mailing lists. These are the most informal auctions of all and are great fun to attend.

I have a lovely old copper wash boiler holding firewood in my living room that is a constant reminder of the value of driving a few extra miles to search out bargains. It's also proof that a little creativity can come in handy at times! Years ago I lived in a small town in the mountains. About twenty-five miles farther up in the hills was a smaller community which every year hosted (are you ready for this?) the Annual Platte River Valley Volunteer Firemen's Auxiliary Auction! I never missed it, because the hard-working ladies of that organization spent all year collecting hundreds upon hundreds of goodies for the August event. There were always a few interesting antiques among the canning jars, electric clocks, and sofa beds. The items up for auction were displayed on long tables in the community churchyard, and nearby was a fine selection of farm machinery, also to be auctioned off at the end of the day.

One year I wore my favorite wide-brimmed pink straw hat as protection from the blazing summer sun. A side benefit was that it made me quite conspicuous among the other bidders. (It pays to have auctioneers recognize you.) Anyway, I bid successfully on several items, and the auctioneer soon realized that "the lady in the pink hat" was a serious customer.

One of the items I planned to bid on was this wash boiler, black with age and tarnish but obviously a fine piece. It was about half-way down one of the long tables. I knew I was not the only person interested in the boiler, as I saw two other women eyeing it covetously.

The auctioneer worked his way down the tables, and by 11:30 a.m. was within 15 feet of the boiler. Then someone called to him, "Hey, Sam, I have to get on my way. Would you mind auctioning off that spreader over there?" Sam, being a nice guy, agreed. He left his place at the table and went over to the farm equipment. By now it was *hot*, and those two women decided to take a quick break at the enticing lemonade table while waiting for Sam to resume selling off the household items. When they left I decided to make my move. I walked over, picked up the boiler, and carried it to the auctioneer. As soon as he finished selling the spreader, I handed the boiler to him and said, "How about putting this up next?" He answered, "Sure, lady, you've been here a long time. No problem." He sold it *right there*, out of the hearing of those at the lemonade table 150 feet away.

The upshot of this is that I got the boiler for $15 while those ladies were quenching their thirst. Needless to say, to avoid mayhem, I packed up my purchases and left quickly. Both of them were bigger than I!

Now, in order to increase the investment you make in the antiques you buy at auctions—no matter which kind you attend—you must maintain a professional attitude. To develop this attitude, emulate the antique dealers you admire.

If you attend local auctions regularly, you begin to recognize local dealers. The enterprising ones never miss a good auction, always looking for bargains to stock their shops. You learn a great deal about buying at auction, for investment, watching the dealers.

Let's walk though the way an astute dealer would act at an average auction in the average American city. For convenience, we'll call this smart cookie "Sally."

Sally arrives at the auction at least a half hour before the scheduled starting time. She immediately goes to the clerk and asks for a "bidding card." In an established auction house the clerk can usually be found at a counter near the floor of the auction. At estate auctions and country auctions the clerk is often found in the front seat of the auctioneer's automobile. The clerk gives Sally a bidding card, a large cardboard card which has a number printed on one side in bold figures. This is the card Sally will hold up to enter a bid. The clerk records Sally's name and address along with the number on her card. This is how the clerk keeps track of what Sally buys during the course of the auction.

The back of this card is blank. It affords an ideal place for Sally to record both the amount she is willing to bid for any item and also her winning bid (should she get the item). There's no charge for the card, so you should always ask for one. No one can enter a bid without a bidding card.

Since Sally is attending an auction in an auction house where seats can be reserved, she has brought along a piece of paper and some cellophane tape. She writes her name on the paper and tapes it to the back of a chair near the front of the house, close to the auctioneer's stand. This informal maneuver reserves that chair for her.

Sally now spends the next half hour inspecting the items that will be put up for bids. All are on display, and each is tagged with a "lot number" for identification. Sally sees three pieces of furniture that she would like to buy. One is an Eastlake-style bed, another a rocker upholstered in red velvet, the third a small marble-topped table, one of a pair. Sally knows that the bed's retail value at this time is around $300, so she's willing to go as high as $150 for it, since it is in fine condition and will need no refinishing. The lot number on the bed is #34.

The rocker is a good example of turn-of-the-century oak furniture, but the upholstery is in bad condition and the wood is obscured with many layers of grimy varnish. It's going to take some work to get this in top condition. The retail value of this rocker— once reconditioned—is around $250. Taking into consideration the time and expense she'll have to go to, Sally decides her top bid on this piece, lot #51, will be $60.

Even though the small table is one of a pair, Sally does not want its mate. Close inspection reveals both a long, deep crack running the full length of the pedestal and cracked marble in one table. The other table is in good condition and worth at least $175, so Sally decides she'll be willing to bid as high as $100 for it, lot #21. Now, if Sally had not examined these tables prior to the sale and noted down the lot numbers, she might not know the difference between the two when the auctioneer held them up for bids. Some auctioneers will make a point of mentioning any defects in an antique, others will not. It's always good insurance to inspect any piece that interests you.

Sally turns her bidding card over and writes:

#34—$150
#51—$60
#21—$100

By this time the auction is ready to start and everyone must take a seat. Only at very informal country auctions and some estate auctions are customers allowed to ramble through the merchandise after the auction starts. Without a prior inspection and lot numbers to guide them, latecomers must bid blindly.

The auction starts, and before long the bed comes up. Sally enters her bids by holding up her card when the auctioneer calls "Do I hear $100?" "Do I hear $125?" and "Do I hear $150?" Holding up the bidding card is a bidder's silent assent to the amount asked by the auctioneer. Since no one tops her bid of $150, Sally gets the bed. Her card number and the figure $150 are noted by the clerk.

Several people are bidding against Sally when the rocker is offered. The bidding is lively and soon reaches the $60 limit Sally decided was her top bid. As much as she wanted that rocker, Sally does not go over her $60 limit. She allows the other party to go higher and win the bid. Remember that Sally wrote down her top bid on the back of the bidding card. This actually serves two purposes. First, it helps her remember both the lot number of the rocker she wanted and the amount she was willing to pay for it. Second, psychologically, it is more difficult to go over a planned bid if you have the predetermined figure you'll be willing to pay *written down.* This is good insurance against auction fever, the disease that makes people bid higher and higher for a coveted item. It is easy to get caught up in the excitement of bidding and end up paying far more for a piece than you should.

The pair of tables does not come up until late afternoon. Sally, along with everyone else, is getting tired by then. The auctioneer places the tables in front of the audience, mentions the lot number of each, and calls for bids. Sally knows which one to bid on, even though from her seat in the third row they look identical. She is the successful bidder for #21 at $90. Someone else ends up bidding the same amount for the second table, a mistake that could have been avoided by careful examination before the auction started.

Since this is all Sally intended to bid on, she goes to the clerk's desk, pays her bill, and arranges to pick up the furniture.

Now, every rule has its exception. And the one I just gave you about not going over a prearranged top bid is one I do occasionally break, but only when I know that I am bidding against a dealer, not a collector. Collectors will often pay almost anything for an especially desirable piece of furniture. Dealers will not. They know what the reasonable price is for that item and will not bid over that figure, usually one-half to one-third of its retail price. They are professional enough to set a specific figure and stick with it. They don't become emotionally involved in the bidding, as collectors often do.

If you find something at an auction that you really want and discover you are bidding *only* against a dealer, you may fudge a bit on your predetermined top bid. A friend, Bill, was able to buy a fine solid-walnut dining table once for just $5 over a dealer's limit by doing this. An elderly woman had sold her home and arranged for the local auctioneer to sell off her furniture and household goods at an estate auction in her backyard. As usual, the auctioneer ran quickly through dozens upon dozens of items of little value (to my friend, anyway). The only thing he really wanted was that table. It was beautiful, and Bill knew it would be a good investment if he could get it at a reasonable price. Dining tables are nearly always in great demand. He decided his top bid would be $200.

Several other people were interested in the table, including a woman Bill recognized as a dealer from a town some fifty miles away. The bidding started at $50 and went up rapidly in increments of $10. One by one the other bidders dropped out until only the dealer and Bill were left. At $180 it was her bid. Bill countered with $190. She hesitated then, and offered $200. Bill's instinct, pretty well-tuned from years of this sort of thing, told him she had set $200 as her limit for that table. The auctioneer turned to Bill and asked for $210. Bill indicated he wouldn't go $210 but would bid $205. The auctioneer accepted that bid and turned back to the dealer, asking for $210. Very unhappily, she shook her head, and Bill got the table.

This woman was a professional. She knew what she could charge for antiques in her shop and what she must pay for them to make a reasonable profit. She set her limits and stuck with them. In your case, though, where you do not have the overhead costs of running a shop or may be buying for long-term investment, you can use a dealer's professionalism to your advantage as Bill did. If you find yourself bidding against someone you know is a dealer, be willing to go *one step* higher than the limit he or she has set. It can pay off in some excellent buys. After some minor refinishing that table increased in value well over twice what Bill paid for it.

This ploy does not always work, of course, especially if you are bidding against a collector. Many individuals who become enamored of a piece of antique furniture at auction will be willing to bid it right up to the current retail value and even beyond. That is their privilege, of course, but it is not the way to make a substantial return on your investment in antiques.

One last word about antique auctions: Bad weather can work in your favor. Casual and nonprofessional buyers are often discouraged from attending a scheduled auction if a storm makes driving there difficult or cold weather makes staying home by the fire more inviting. This can be your chance to pick up some real bargains. The dealers will nearly always show up, regardless of rain, sleet, snow, or high water, but remember, they set wholesale price limits on themselves. Button up your overcoat and go! For a few dollars more you just might be able to bid your way to some fine antique furniture.

GARAGE SALES

My friends are often incredulous when I tell them that I find many of my antique bargains, especially those in need of much TLC, at garage sales. "You're joking!" they almost always reply. In answer, I point to some lovely picture frames and mirrors on my walls, to a delicate hall tree with a round mirror, and especially to an exquisite English mahogany desk in my study. All of these now look as though they came from fine antique shops. Yet each found its way to my home by way of one garage sale or another. Many other, equally beautiful, pieces have been sold or given to my children as gifts.

Never discount the lowly garage sale as a source of antiques to renovate! This is frequently where you will find your biggest and best bargains. To make your hunt successful, though, you must develop a good strategy and be persistent.

Your strategy begins by studying the classified listings under "Garage Sales" in your local paper the night before you plan to go out, usually on Friday night, since most garage sales are held on weekends. Look through all the listings, circling any that have the word "antiques" somewhere in the ad. Also, look especially for any that say the person giving the sale is cleaning out "forty years accumulation of junk" or some such wording. Every once in a while I'll come upon a little gem at one of these sales. These can be especially productive if the ads give addresses in older, middle-class neighborhoods. These will be people who have lived in their homes for many, many years, and these homes have the big attics and full basements that are conducive to holding onto possessions. Most residents of suburbia move too frequently to accumulate much, and storage space is usually at a premium in their homes.

Go back over the sales you've circled and make out a route. Time is of the essence in finding bargains in antiques at garage sales because many other people have the same idea that you have. You can beat them to the punch by getting to the goodies first.

My routine is to plot a route with a colored felt pen. I mark the sale closest to my house "1" and continue numbering those farther away "2," "3," etc. I drive to "1" first, then on to "2" and so on down the list. That way I don't waste time backtracking all over town.

Surprisingly, the best buys are not usually at the home where the ad lists "antiques" in bold letters as the main attraction. Often you'll find beautiful furniture at these sales, but it will be expertly restored and the prices asked are retail. I think much of this furniture was bought at *other* garage sales and refinished with the express purpose of reselling it for a profit.

However, I *love* those sales where the ads list "antiques" buried in small type right along with a laundry list of old records, Avon bottles, ski boots, and kitchen sinks. Almost without exception I find these to be my best hunting grounds.

That's the way I came by my beautiful old English desk. The list of items offered at that garage sale contained everything from baby clothes to a gun rack. But deep inside the list were two simple words, "antique desk." Frankly, I thought it would be a child's school desk at best. So when I walked into the chilly garage and looked around I was a bit disappointed not to see even that on display.

"Have you sold your antique desk?" I asked the homeowner. "No, it's inside if you'd like to see it," he replied.

I followed him into the house and into a back room that was obviously the spare room, since it wasn't decorated nearly as well as the rest of the house. "There it is," my host said, pointing to a far wall of the room. I could not believe my eyes. The desk was one of the most original I had ever seen. A full 50 inches wide and 25 inches deep, it stood 60 inches high and was graced with a top of finely grained pink marble. The back, which rose from that marble top, boasted another piece of the marble and a deeply beveled mirror. On either side of the mirror were shelves to hold candlesticks.

I caught my breath and asked, "How much do you want for the desk?" He mentioned a figure that I knew was less than half its value. Upon closer examination I discovered that one decorative finial was missing and that the marble top was cracked in several places. The owner agreed that it would cost something to put the desk in top condition and reduced the price accordingly. Gratefully, I accepted this offer and gave him a check before someone else discovered this lovely desk. It's now one of my proudest possessions and never fails to cause awed comment from my guests.

Once you have your route planned you're ready to start out on your antique hunt. And do begin early! If the first sale is scheduled to begin at 8:00 a.m., you should *be there* by 7:50 at the latest. Look the merchandise over carefully and quickly and buy anything that looks promising, then drive on to the next sale on your list. Don't linger. This may not be quite as much fun as a neighborly chat with the other shoppers, but remember, in order to find the bargains in antiques *first*, you must *get* there first.

One important word on strategy: If you see something you are even remotely interested in—pick it up! You may still be trying to decide whether or not a wobbly frame, for instance, is worth buying, but as long as you have it in your hands, it is potentially yours. The Code of the Garage Sale is that possession is nine-tenths of the law. You may decide after a few moments' inspection that the frame is really circa 1965 and not the Art Deco treasure you thought at first. You can always put it back on the table for someone else to examine. But as long as it was in your hands you had first dibs on it.

My friend Joanne learned this lesson the hard way. She arrived at a garage sale early and immediately spotted a charming little table with spiraled pedestal legs. She bent closer to try to get her bifocals in focus to read the price tag. Before Joanne got there, though, a cagier shopper picked up the table and walked off with it. She got it for $10! If Joanne had picked it *up* to read the price tag, she would have had squatter's rights to the table and it would be in her home now.

Always go to garage sales with plenty of change and small bills. Many people who hold garage sales do not have enough change and dollar bills at the very beginning of the day. They're often confronted right at the start of the sale with people wanting to buy and having only $10 and $20 bills to buy with. So, you can frequently get them to lower a price a bit (thereby increasing your percentage of investment growth) by offering coins and dollar bills in payment for an article.

I've also discovered that cash comes in handy when an owner first refuses to lower the price of an item. I once came upon a nice high-backed chair in excellent condition at a garage sale. The price on it was $35. I asked the owner if he would take less. He said, "No, the price is firm." So, I reached into my wallet and pulled out five $5 bills. I held them out to him and asked, "Would you take $25 cash for the chair?" After a moment he said yes and sold me the chair!

There is a psychological advantage in *offering* actual cash instead of talking about it. This maneuver doesn't always work, of course, but I've used it successfully often enough to be able to recommend that you try it, too.

Approached scientifically (and that's the only way to find the real bargains) going to garage sales is not the time-consuming activity that going to auctions certainly can be. The best buys in inexpensive antiques go very quickly. Remember my warning to start early and get there first! I am almost always through with my list and back home by 10:00 on a Saturday morning. And it is a rare day that I don't drive back into my *own* garage with at least one or two treasures!

FLEA MARKETS

Flea markets are really just big garage sales that are held by many dealers instead of by individual homeowners. The same rules that apply at garage sales can be used profitably when searching for antiques at flea markets.

Arrive early while the different dealers are still setting up their tables and arranging their merchandise. This means *before* the scheduled opening time. If you should see a really desirable item, you just might be able to buy it then before the crowds arrive.

Move quickly through the selling area to assess which dealers might have any stock you'd be interested in buying.

Carry cash and come prepared to dicker. Good-natured bargaining is the name of the game at most flea markets, and you should at least try to get a dealer to lower his or her price.

The real difference between garage sales and flea markets is that dealers at the latter will often trade merchandise, both among themselves and with their customers. It is entirely possible to buy a picture frame from one dealer, for instance, walk a few tables down the aisle, and trade the frame to another dealer for something of greater value to you.

Many towns have regularly scheduled flea markets that have operated every weekend for years. They draw dealers and customers from miles around. While they are not the best sources for antiques, they're certainly worth looking into.

SECONDHAND STORES

Secondhand stores are a minor source of antiques for restoration. But lightning does strike once in a while, so don't discount them. The big advantage you'll find here is that most secondhand furniture dealers are just that, they're not too knowledgeable about or interested in antiques. They simply want to move the merchandise out of their shops as quickly as possible. On the rare occasion that they acquire a good old buffet or chest of drawers, they will proba- bly sell it to you for the same price they would a ten-year-old one that really *is* just used furniture.

Your best hunting grounds are secondhand stores in rural areas or very small towns. They are off the regular routes of the dealers, who are always on the lookout for bargains in antiques. And few serious collectors will take the time to scour the countryside on the outside chance they'll find a gem for their collections.

Considering the price of gasoline today and the value of one's time, I wouldn't suggest that you invest too much of either in checking out secondhand stores. However, anytime you're driving through a small town on vacation or business, by all means look for the local secondhand stores. A few minutes' detour off the highway and down a back street on such a mission has proved profitable for me on one or two occasions.

This chapter has listed four common places you can search for antiques in need of restoration—auctions, garage sales, flea mar- kets, and secondhand stores. You'll probably find auctions to be your best source. They are for me and for most other men and women who are trying to increase their investment in antiques. However, you may well be able to ferret out other markets. For instance, I once discovered a lovely old beveled mirror at a hotel that was being converted to office space.

A friend found a rare triple-press oak rocker in the attic of an antique shop and bought it for one-third its value. The owner of the shop had been intending to refinish it for years and sold it because he finally decided he'd never have the time.

I admired a truly magnificent rolltop desk in a lawyer's office once. The gentlemen told me that he prized it second only to his wife. He had found the desk in several dozen pieces in a barn and spent an entire winter cleaning, repairing, and reassembling it to its former opulence. He had paid $10 for the boxes of pieces, and when I saw the desk, it was easily worth three hundred times that.

Even more important to him than the monetary increase, though, was his obvious pride and satisfaction in having restored this superb and most elegant example of fine office furniture.

So, whether at a city auction attended by hundreds of eager buyers or in a dusty barn on a lonely ranch in Wyoming, the bargains in antique furniture definitely are there. And you can find them, just as I and hundreds of others do.

To make this delightful hobby/business both fun and profitable, you must learn to recognize the antiques that have real potential for rapid investment growth. The next chapter will help you begin to acquire this important knowledge.

THE "REAL" ANTIQUES: THE COLONIAL PERIOD TO THE VICTORIAN PERIOD

What is an antique, anyway? After all, "antique" means "old," doesn't it? Yes, certainly, but "old" is an abstract and highly relative term. I've heard teenagers refer to anyone over thirty-five as old. Yet my sixtyish aunt once remarked to me (upon hearing I had just reached thirty-five), "My, my, how nice to be so young!" So, antique, like old, means different things to different people.

Those who live on the East Coast of the United States, where our country is the oldest, generally consider a piece of furniture an antique if it predates 1825 or so. In the lower South, where a Camelot-like civilization flourished during the mid-nineteenth century, "antique" and "Victorian" are almost synonymous terms. Out here in the Wild West, where I live, however, any piece of furniture built around the *close* of the nineteenth century is a bona fide antique! This part of the country is so new that very little besides teepees and buffalo robes existed much before that.

The United States government at one time declared an official antique to be any piece of furniture made before 1830. That date is the approximate year powered furniture-making machines were perfected. Faced with the passage of time, though, the Congress in

1966 ruled that a piece of furniture had only to be one hundred years old to be an authentic antique. So, as this is written, any piece of furniture made prior to the closing decade of the nineteenth century is officially an antique.

As mentioned earlier, this book is not intended to show you how to buy (and perhaps sell) those exquisitely lovely early pieces that bring four- and five-figure prices at the fancier auctions and antique shops. We'll be working almost exclusively with the more readily available pieces that are a hundred years or so old. It certainly will be to your advantage, though, to be able to recognize all the major American furniture styles of the last few centuries. This knowledge will add immensely to your own enjoyment of good furniture. And who knows, you just might get lucky someday and discover a treasure trove of beauties that will make not only your fortune but your reputation as an antiques expert! Toward that end, this chapter and the next describe the several furniture styles that are a part of our American heritage. Some are unquestionably antiques. Some are borderline cases—all depending upon your point of view.

COLONIAL PERIOD—EARLY TO LATE SEVENTEENTH CENTURY

The earliest settlers to the American colonies made only the crudest sort of furniture. Rough and strictly utilitarian, it bore little resemblance to the Jacobean styles they had left behind in England and Europe. (The term "Jacobean" comes from the Latin word "Jacobus" for James, and refers to the period during which James I was on the throne of England.)

A few examples of this early period, pieces constructed around the middle of the seventeenth century, are on display in several East Coast museums. Old inventories and wills give us a still better idea of the way the first Americans furnished their homes. Settlers in rural areas away from the cities used plainer, simpler furniture than their city cousins. Well-to-do city folk, however, hired turners and joiners (early terms for the craftsmen who later were called cabinetmakers) who emulated their English peers of that period.

By mid-seventeenth century these men were beginning to turn out furniture that closely resembled the heavy medieval styles favored in England during the reigns of Queen Elizabeth I and King James I. The furniture was elaborate, massive, and ornate with bulbous table legs and deeply carved cabinet fronts.

Simple stools and benches were more popular than chairs in Colonial homes. A settle was often placed beside the fireplace. This was a long bench with a high back to shield the person sitting there from cold drafts. It also captured as much heat as possible from the fireplace.

Houses were small, so homeowners were always interested in any piece of furniture which could do double duty or could be folded away when not in use. So, many homes had gateleg tables which had a fixed top in the center attached to a frame of legs and sturdy stretchers. These legs and stretchers were carved in the better pieces. Two large drop leaves hung on either side of the center section, ready to be lifted and supported on movable legs that swung out on either side of the table.

Virtually every home of any substance had, by the end of the seventeenth century, a press cupboard and/or a court cupboard for storage. The press cupboard was a fairly simple enclosed chest used to store clothing or household linen. The court cupboard was more elaborate, with open areas to display cherished silver plate and precious utensils. Most of these large pieces of furniture were Tudor in style, heavily carved and decorated in the motifs of medieval England. Some, however, showed simpler and straighter lines, influenced by the native designs brought to the new country by the many immigrants from Sweden.

Beds by the end of that century were probably high-posted affairs that dominated the small bedrooms. Undoubtedly, they were hung with curtains to close out the night air.

What little we know about the furniture of this period shows us that it was stiff, formal, and probably miserably uncomfortable. Puritan philosophy still held sway in the colonies, with its strict religious code and abhorrence of anything that smacked of "worldly" pleasure. Ease and comfort were definitely not the major criteria for the furniture of the time.

The favored woods were those that grew most plentifully in the forests—oak and pine, although walnut, ash, hickory, maple, apple, and cherry were used when and where available.

WILLIAM AND MARY PERIOD—LATE SEVENTEENTH CENTURY TO EARLY EIGHTEENTH CENTURY

William of Orange and his Queen, Mary, followed the hated despot James II onto the throne of England in 1689. Their arrival from Holland was like a breath of fresh air. More than ready for a change, England quickly adopted the new ideas William and Mary brought with them.

The new monarchs soon moved out much of the stolid English furniture from their apartments and installed their own more cheerful and elegant pieces. Lighter, more graceful interior decoration was part of their contribution to English life. The royal court followed suit, and then the English people as a whole. At about the same time Dutch colonists introduced the same styles into the American colonies. So it was inevitable that in America the massive Tudor furniture of the latter seventeenth century should be replaced by the more comfortable and attractive designs inspired by the Dutch monarchs on the British throne.

Life was also getting a bit easier for the colonists, and this soon was reflected in more discretionary furniture. Letter writing, for instance, increased, and the long table that served in most homes for food preparation, dining, children's lessons, family conferences, and everything else was often in use and not amenable to long sessions with a quill pen. Besides one needed a place to store that pen, ink, and paper. To fill this need, cabinetmakers began offering small desks. The first were simple desks-on-frames, little more than boxes with slanted tops resting on frames with four legs. The slanted top (the writing surface) opened on hinges, usually at the upper edge, and writing materials were stored inside. In time cabinetmakers began putting the hinges on the lower edge of the writing surface instead of the upper edge. Thus, the top opened down instead of up, and the inside became the writing surface. This was supported, when lowered, on sliding rails that pulled out of the desk itself. Soon, drawers were added to the lower frame, and finally, a bank of small pigeonholes and drawers was installed in the upper section.

Small and medium-sized tables found their way into these homes, too, for the first time. Colonists used them for playing cards, serving tea, and displaying treasured objects, all embellishments of a more leisurely way of life.

Rather ornate dressing tables also came into vogue around the beginning of the eighteenth century. Typically, a dressing table was a small table with a shallow center drawer and two deeper side drawers. The table often had an elaborately shaped apron and usually rested on four turned legs with X-shaped cross stretchers (the horizontal braces between legs used to strengthen a piece). Similar tables were used for preparing food. With slate, marble, or tile tops, they were impervious to heat and resistant to knife cuts. These tables were called slate or slab tables.

The high chest was a variation of the dressing or slate table. Here an attractive chest with three or four tiers of drawers was attached to the top of the small table. More drawers were eventually added to the bottom half of this piece of furniture, resulting in a chest-on-chest of drawers that became known as the highboy. This tall piece of furniture replaced the press and court cupboards for storage of linens and clothing.

This movement toward more vertical styles was a distinct hallmark of the William and Mary period. In addition to the new tall chests of drawers, beds had higher posts and chairs had higher backs. These taller, more graceful designs were all indicative of the delicacy in furniture which William and Mary favored and encouraged.

Caned seats, an Oriental innovation, appeared on side chairs about this time, and the immensely popular wing chair developed. This chair, which is now a classic design, was the first easy chair. Well-padded and fully upholstered, this chair was the first real breakthrough in seating comfort. Like the settle of a few years earlier, it also served to ward off drafts in homes where the only heat came from an open fireplace.

Most of the furniture built during this period was more comfortable and attractive than that of early Colonial days. Cabinetmakers began using more walnut and maple than before, and they added a delicacy to their work with fine veneers, inlay, arched panels, and generally less ponderous turnings.

The wealthier colonists even began ordering cabinetmakers to adorn their new tables and high chests with gilt stencils and fine lacquer work. The ponderousness of Tudor England was giving way to a new elegance and individuality as men and women established their roots in America.

QUEEN ANNE PERIOD—EARLY TO MID-EIGHTEENTH CENTURY

This period of American furniture, named for Queen Anne of England, who held the throne from 1702 until 1714, actually flourished long after her reign ended. And from old prints and inventories it is obvious that life became increasingly easier for the colonists as the century advanced. Few innovative furniture forms were introduced during these years, but several of the earlier William and Mary styles were modified to accommodate a more leisurely way of life. We find more sophisticated folding card tables and delicate tea tables, for instance, than a few years before. Those tea tables, whether rectangular or round, almost invariably had a "dished," or recessed, top.

During the first quarter of the eighteenth century, cabinetmakers began using the cyma curve, a form which got its name from the Greek word for wave form. A classic shape, the cyma curve is a double curve, simple and elegant. It eventually became the dominant motif of the period, seen in pediments, dressing table aprons, and chair backs, but most notably in the distinctive cabriole leg.

The balance of two curves produced a stability that belied its delicate appearance, and helped to make the cabriole leg a hallmark of furniture design throughout much of the eighteenth century. It appeared on virtually every table, chest, and chair produced during the period. The lower portion usually ended in a thick pad or shaped foot. Some designers preferred the more ornate claw and ball foot.

Architects and furniture designers during the Queen Anne pe-

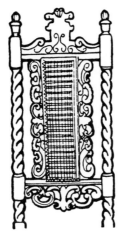

Caning, carving and spiral
twist (Stuart, second
half seventeenth century)

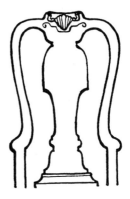

Solid Splat (Queen Anne
and early Georgian)

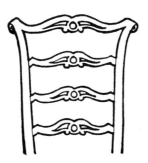

Ladder Back (Chippendale,
mid-eighteenth century)

Wheel Back (Hepplewhite,
late eighteenth century)

Gothick (Chippendale,
mid-eighteenth century)

Ribband Back (Chippendale,
mid-eighteenth century)

Chair Backs

riod also became entranced with the shell as a decorating motif. And it soon was as ubiquitous as the cabriole leg. Many fine homes of the period still boast elaborate shell carving and molding over fireplaces and inside cupboards. Following suit, cabinetmakers embellished the front panels of chests, knees of table and chair legs, pediments of all kinds, and chair backs with classic, open shell carvings.

Inlay and marquetry faded from style, but skilled cabinetmakers used much lacquer and veneer to decorate the plain surfaces of their furniture. Carving was not quite so heavy as a few years before, with far more restrained paneling and molding on the flat surfaces. Japanning, a method of applying a Japanese-inspired lacquer with a hard, glossy finish, came into vogue during the Queen Anne period. It usually featured brightly colored and fanciful birds and fruits decorating a black background. Sometimes animals, human figures, and stylized oriental buildings literally covered the larger and more expensive tall chests. The effect was one of opulence and wealth.

As the period advanced, cabinetmakers began to eschew the flat top on case pieces for the more elaborate broken pediment, often punctuated with central finials. These vase-shaped carved decorations were a final touch of elegance. Almost all the surviving secretaries of this period, in fact, are topped with the broken pediment, and it has come to symbolize, as much as do the cabriole leg and shell motif, the graceful Queen Anne period. Along the same line, chairmakers began inserting flat sections of wood, called splats, into the backs of their chairs. Replacing the spindles of earlier days, these splats were often cut in the shape of fiddles or classical vases. Also, with an eye to the comfort that seemed to be ever more important to this generation, these chair backs were often shaped to conform more closely to the curve of the human spine.

Cabinetmakers favored walnut during this era, with maple and cherry close seconds. Mahogany was introduced to the colonies during the first few years of the eighteenth century but did not take hold as a major wood for fine furniture until the latter part of the century.

An important addition to the history of furniture in America occurred during the Queen Anne period. It did not in any way reflect that style, but did turn out to be totally endearing, enduring, and firmly wedged in the hearts of the men and women of this country. This was the Windsor chair.

WINDSOR CHAIRS Around 1725 one of the most durable chair designs ever devised arrived in America from its native England. This was the Windsor, and inventive Yankee chair makers quickly took to its simple, sturdy form. Basically, the Windsor is an all-wood chair with a solid seat shaped for comfortable sitting, legs which spread out at about a 20-degree angle, and approximately twelve to twenty-four slender, straight spindles in the back. A comfortable chair, it seems to fit well in just about any setting from country cottage to millionaire's mansion. Perhaps that is the secret of its success. No other individual chair style, except perhaps the wing chair, has retained its consistent popularity through the years.

Thomas Jefferson loved the Windsor chair, and historians believe he sat in one when signing the Declaration of Independence. We do know he bought forty-eight of them in black and gold to seat his many illustrious guests at Monticello. Benjamin Franklin ordered twenty-four Windsors at one time and specified that they be painted white. George Washington bought twenty-seven for Mount Vernon, but we don't know his preference in color.

Early Windsors were nearly always painted, often green, red, or yellow. They were humble chairs, usually made from a motley collection of woods, and the paint disguised the mismatched parts. Poplar or pine, both softwoods and easily shaped, were often used for the saddle seats. The legs, spindles, and arms might be beech, hickory, maple, ash, or any other hardwood, and often a combination of two or more.

These early Windsor chairs were put together without nails or screws. In fact, they owe their sturdiness to a unique construction method. First the legs and spindles were turned from seasoned wood. The chair maker then set these pieces into well-fitting holes in plank seats which had been carved from *green* wood. In time the green wood dried and shrank, gripping the ends of the legs and spindles with all the tenacity of a bear trap. This made a first-rate bond that just didn't let go with time. Later models, though, were made by conventional methods with glue and screws and usually of one wood throughout.

Windsors come in all forms—fan-backed, straight-backed, curved-backed. The most valuable for the antique collector are those with two to four braces behind the back spindles. Springing from an extension of the seat at the rear, they rise to meet the upper edge of the back, forming quite an effective brace.

The value and quality of a Windsor chair is also determined by the number of spindles in its back. The very earliest, and, therefore, rarest, Windsors often had eleven spindles. Later, chair makers began making them with seven and nine spindles. These are still quite valuable. We often find Windsors made in the late nineteenth century, though, with as few as five spindles. These are fairly common and don't command very high prices.

CHIPPENDALE PERIOD—MID- TO LATE EIGHTEENTH CENTURY

Thomas Chippendale was an English cabinetmaker whose styles had tremendous influence on American furniture during the mid- to late eighteenth century and for years afterward. Some controversy exists as to just how original the designs were that came from his London shop. One school of thought says he shamelessly plagiarized the ideas of his contemporaries. Another claims that his hired apprentices and assistants were actually the creative genius behind his work. On the other hand, much evidence exists to say Chippendale himself actually designed at least the major portion of the work attributed to him. Regardless, he was a giant among eighteenth-century cabinetmakers and made an indelible impact both in his native England and in America.

The furniture he sold to eager Englishmen and -women was actually a blend of many styles, including Georgian, William and Mary, Queen Anne, Rococo, and Gothic, and was influenced by the Chinese, Spanish, and French. Some of this furniture did find its way to the colonies. However, most of the "Chippendale" which survives here today is actually Chippendale-inspired. Hundreds of Colonial cabinetmakers quickly recognized the beauty of Chippendale's styles and adapted those ideas in their own workshops for their own customers. The American adaptations were

Chinese (Chippendale, mid-eighteenth century)

Shield Back (Hepplewhite, late eighteenth century)

Stuffed Oval (Adam, late eighteenth century)

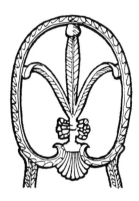

Prince of Wales Plumes (Hepplewhite, late eighteenth century)

Sheraton (late eighteenth century)

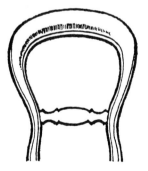

Balloon Back (Victorian, mid-nineteenth century)

More Chair Backs

quite a bit simpler than the English originals, though, and almost totally Georgian and Queen Anne derivations.

The highboy (chest of four drawers on top of a matching aproned dressing table) continued its popularity in America throughout the Chippendale period, even though it was passé in England. Invariably, these Chippendale highboys were topped with a broken pediment and finials carved in the shape of vases. Many had fan- or shell-shaped inserts below the pediment or at the joining of the top and lower sections.

An innovation during this period was the kneehole dressing table or chest of drawers. A refinement of the earlier dressing table, it had a bank of drawers on either side of the open kneehole, with the two joined by a small center drawer.

For the first time, too, we find cabinetmakers producing the elaborate breakfront bookcases. Most of these large pieces of furniture had glazed upper sections, some with arched panels, and many topped with the broken pediment. The lower section might be a bank of drawers with a central writing section, similar to those found in secretaries. Or it could have wooden doors, often veneered with fine woods cut into fanciful patterns to display the lovely grains.

The pembroke table was another newcomer to the growing list of small tables being produced for early Americans. Often used as a breakfast table for two, the pembroke was a simple rectangular table with short drop leaves and usually a small drawer for storing cutlery. Most often the legs were square, with cross stretchers. Sometimes the stretchers were decorated with elaborate openwork carving; sometimes they were quite plain.

During the former Queen Anne period tea tables often had a dished, or slightly recessed, top. Chippendale cabinetmakers refined this feature a bit by turning that low ridge into a fancy fluted piecrust-like rim. We find this embellishment almost exclusively on round, often three-legged tables. The legs of these delicate tables were usually deeply carved with some of the most elaborate patterns of the period.

Nearly all side chairs and armchairs of this period had splats instead of rails, but during the Chippendale era they were far more ornate than before. Frequently pierced in graceful designs, they echoed the cyma curve, which continued to be a favorite motif with American cabinetmakers. Most Chippendale-inspired furniture, in fact, made free use of graceful curves, including the cabriole leg. Most often that leg terminated in an elaborate claw and ball foot. Some furniture makers, though, continued to use the simpler pad, club, web, or drake foot of previous years. Quite typical of the period, too, were the many acanthus leaves, swags, shells, and scrolls that decorated chests, desks, highboys, and breakfronts.

By this time mahogany was being imported into the young colonies in great quantities from Santo Domingo and Honduras, and it was the favored wood of sophisticated cabinetmakers of the period. The native woods—walnut, maple, cherry, pine, and poplar—still appeared, though they were used primarily by craftsmen in small towns and rural areas.

THE ROCKING CHAIR Like the steadfast Windsor chair, which developed during the Queen Anne period but was not a part of it, a furniture maverick appeared during the Chippendale period. This was the ubiquitous rocking chair.

The rocking chair is one piece of furniture which actually has its roots in the United States. The idea has been credited to Benjamin Franklin, our master inventor. No one knows for sure, though, who first came up with the idea of putting runners on chairs, or when the rocking chair was first made. However, all evidence points to a date of around 1760. Regardless of the exact date, over two centuries of Americans have rocked their babies to sleep in this delightful chair.

The earliest rocking chairs were not built as rocking chairs but were converted by adding runners to the legs of regular side chairs. At first chair makers and homeowners simply cut a notch into the inner or outer side of the lower 2 or 3 inches of the chair legs. The runners were then fitted into these notches. These early runners were quite thin and deep, some were little wider than ¼ inch but were 3 inches from one edge to the other. Understandably, they were known as carpet cutters!

Another indication of a conversion, other than the obvious addition of a runner to an existing chair leg, is the shape of the leg.

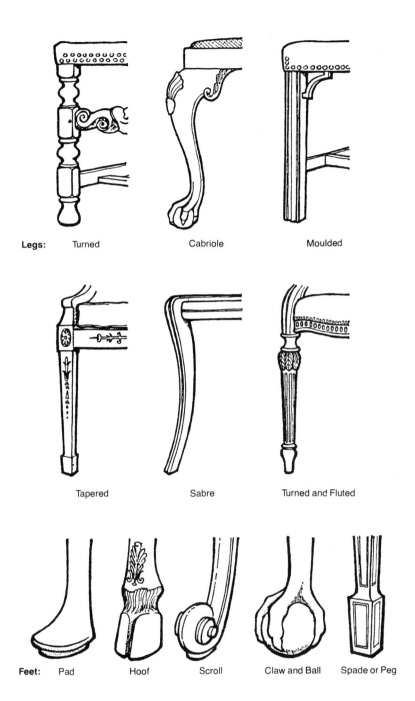

Legs: Turned   Cabriole   Moulded

Tapered   Sabre   Turned and Fluted

Feet: Pad   Hoof   Scroll   Claw and Ball   Spade or Peg

Chair Legs and Feet

Most chairs have a slightly tapered leg, wider at the upper edge than at the lower. Side chairs converted to rocking chairs will still have this tapered leg, of course. Later on when chair makers began building chairs specifically as rockers, they built legs with essentially the same circumference from top to bottom. They then cut the notch into the center of the lower edge of the leg and slipped the runner into that notch. A pair of pins or dowels was then driven through the legs and the runners to secure them onto the chair.

Appalled at the destruction of carpeting, chair makers began making runners with the approximate dimensions we see today, about 1 inch wide and 1½ to 2 inches deep. At the same time they discarded the notch system and began applying the runners directly to the base of the chair leg.

Regardless of the way runners were applied, though, rocking chairs were made in every conceivable style and size. Some were pure Windsor. Others were the distinctive Boston rocker and Hitchcock rocker. We find Sheraton-influence rockers and Duncan Phyfe-influence rockers. Victorian rocking chairs abound, as do the charming little low-seated sewing or nursing rocking chairs. All found a place in the homes and hearts of Americans.

FEDERAL OR CLASSICAL PERIOD—LATE EIGHTEENTH CENTURY TO EARLY NINETEENTH CENTURY

Many designers whose names are household words may be grouped under the general heading of the Federal or Classical period in American furniture. Among others, this includes Hepplewhite, Sheraton, and Duncan Phyfe. Also a part of this era are the styles known as Empire and Directoire. No one particular motif can be said to typify this era of great change in the United States. It was a blend of many styles, covering some fifty vastly disparate years from shortly after the American Revolution until the ascent of Victoria to the throne of England.

The style known as Duncan Phyfe was the only one which originated in the new United States. The others had crossed the Atlantic from England and Europe. After winning their independence, Americans were ready and willing to throw off the old and take on the new. In reacting against the rococo curves, the Gothic ostentatiousness, and the pseudo-Chinese influences of the previous half century, they joyfully embraced the straighter, more classical lines of "the new look."

The curving lines of the cabriole leg with its pad and/or claw foot all but disappeared as chair and table legs became slender and tapered. Ornate shell and leaf carvings were replaced with reeding, decorative molding characterized by several slender, rounded reed-like shapes as on a column, and simple turnings. A relatively plain oval, shield, or heart-shaped back appeared on side chairs, creating a more delicate and airy design than the formal pierced and carved Chippendale splats. The elegant and elaborate highboys and lowboys became unfashionable, and homeowners went back to storing their clothing and linens in plainer chests of drawers.

Curves were gentle and restrained, often seen in a slightly bowed front on chests and desks. Instead of ornate carvings we see more simple lyres, urns, and inlaid ovals as motifs on furniture of this period.

Probably the two most important innovations of this period were the commode and the sideboard. The commode was a small chest, usually about 3 feet high. The most beautiful examples were often semicircular and intended for use in the parlor. They had drawers and shelves to store the niceties of upper-middle-class living of the time. More commonly, the commode was built for the bedroom and served as a washstand. It had a marble or wood top with drawers and shelves below for linens and toiletries.

The sideboard, though, is almost a trademark of this period in furniture. Most were built in three sections with four to six legs and had drawers for cutlery, and shelves behind paneled doors for china, linens, and silverware. Many had a serpentine front, the new undulating style achieved with a series of gentle convex and concave curves.

The American people developed a great deal of empathy for France during this time, since the French people had recently fought for their liberty from a tyrannical monarchy. Therefore,

Mounts: Axe Drop (mid-seventeenth century)

Swan Neck with shaped pierced plate (early eighteenth century)

Pear Drop (late seventeenth century)

Swan Neck (Queen Anne)

Lion Mask (Regency)

Pierced back plate with Chinese influence (mid-eighteenth century)

Neo-classical (Adam)

Prince of Wales Plumes (late eighteenth century)

French Rococo (mid-eighteenth century)

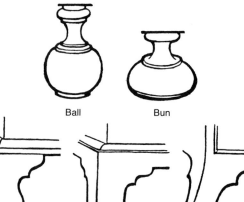

Supports:

Ball

Bun

Ogee

Bracket

Splayed Bracket

Furniture Mounts and Supports

when France embraced the rather austere style known as Directoire, around 1790, Americans happily took the new ideas to their hearts. Greatly influenced by Napoleon, this style had an almost military ambiance, with sofa legs that resembled sabers, and table legs shaped like flaming torches. Other frequent motifs were wreaths, laurel branches, stars, rosettes, battle axes, shields, and palm leaves. Wherever possible, designers worked a patriotic red, white, and blue color scheme into a painted cabinet, desk, or chest. In America, an eagle, the symbol of the new nation, topped thousands upon thousands of mirror frames and pediments, and often served as an ornamental support for occasional tables.

Within a few years the spartan designs of the Directoire period gave way to a heavier style which became known as American Empire. Less graceful than its parent, the Empire styles of France, this massive and stolid furniture lacked much of the beauty and elegance of Directoire designs. Beds were often fashioned with huge sleigh-like headboards and footboards, and brass hardware was frequently molded in the shape of lions' heads with rings for pulls. We find many carved pineapples, animal feet, and elaborate cornices on furniture of the second and third decade of the nineteenth century.

About the same time, both Europe and America rediscovered the classics. No longer did fashionable men and women look for freshness and innovation in their furniture. Creativity went out the door as antiquity came in. The public demanded furniture, silverware, clothing, houses, even outhouses, that duplicated the possessions of those who lived in Greece, Rome, and Egypt thousands of years before. Suddenly "Doric," "Ionic," and "Corinthian" became household words. The simple taper disappeared from table and chair legs, and ornate columns appeared emulating the columns which supported the roofs of ancient temples. The motifs on frieze-like borders along table aprons and around mirrors could have enhanced the Roman Senate or an Eyptian altar.

Since this vogue for the classics ran parallel to that of other, more developmental styles, we frequently find one element superimposed on another. Pier tables, for instance, those low pieces built to stand between two long windows, could have a top and lower shelf that was pure Directoire, yet boast lovely Grecian figures as supports for the upper sections. A pair of winged sphinx might serve as arm supports for a chair whose back was pure Duncan Phyfe.

The entire Federal period, in fact, was one of transition. One style melded into another and overlay another as many talented designers worked at satisfying the demands of the time.

VICTORIAN PERIOD—EARLY TO LATE NINETEENTH CENTURY

Some of the furniture produced during the nineteenth century was undeniably in the worst possible taste, replete with as many scrolls, carved motifs, rococo curves, and general embellishments as a hardworking cabinetmaker could tack on or gouge out of the wood. Some of the furniture produced during this period still showed the restraint of earlier periods, though, with simple lines and near-classical ambiance. And there is no getting around the fact that furniture of this period is certainly the most available of all in today's antiques market. The trick for the collector or investor is to weed out the good from the awful.

Shaker furniture flourished during the nineteenth century, but it can in no way be described as fitting into the mode of most Victorian styles. The religious sect which developed this sturdy and simple furniture came to the United States from England about the time of the American Revolution. Hardworking and thrifty, they prospered and by the mid-nineteenth century some eighteen Shaker communities existed throughout the Northeast.

The Shakers were an industrious and business-like people who sold their products far outside the realm of their own communities. Their furniture, especially, clearly defined their own belief in the virtue of the simple life. It was attractive, functional, sturdy, and quite devoid of ornament. In many ways, Shaker styles are similar to those of the American Colonial period.

In time the popular Shaker furniture became standard throughout the various Shaker communities and was patented for protection from imitators. Today, therefore, we can identify as "Shaker" the furniture these people made. One of the most popular and comfortable Shaker pieces is the rocking chair with high ladder back, rush seat, and simple tapered finials. Some of their candle stands seem strikingly modern and blend well with twentieth-century furnishings. They have round tops, usually three legs, and those legs are often shaped into a restrained cyma curve.

Many of the small worktables had tops that extended several inches past the supporting apron, and most had a drawer for cutlery set into one end. The trestle tables which were the central feature of Shaker living and dining rooms were rectangular, with pedestals at either end. The table had a flat stretcher between the pedestals, often placed quite high, sometimes just inches below the top of the table itself.

Shaker cabinetmakers preferred the simpler native woods of their adopted country—maple, cherry, butternut, birch, and pine.

Interestingly enough, another small voice for good taste and simplicity made itself heard quite early in the Victorian age. This was the unpretentious style known as spool furniture. These casual designs were first introduced in *Godey's Lady's Book* around 1815 and remained popular for some fifty years. Turned out en masse by both large Eastern factories and local cabinetmakers, spool furniture resembled a series of spools, buttons, or balls strung together like beads on a necklace. The improved lathes of the time could turn the symmetrical spools quickly and efficiently, and we find them used on every conceivable piece of furniture, but most prominently as bedposts. Though produced during the Victorian age, spool furniture is really not Victorian in feeling. It is more a by-product of the more formal styles popular during the late seventeenth century.

Cabinetmakers produced spool furniture in every wood from walnut to cherry. The less desirable woods such as pine and poplar were usually stained to emulate walnut, rosewood, or mahogany, the most fashionable cabinet woods of the Victorian age.

Victoria came to the throne of England in 1837. Though she was a romantic, stuffy young woman, her values quickly became the values of her time. Victoria's reign began just as the Classical period was declining, so many of the excesses of the first years of the nineteenth century are evident in the early Victorian period. During this transition time many furniture makers were trying to combine different styles into one piece of furniture. It wasn't at all unusual for a wardrobe to boast a French Renaissance top with elegant gold stenciling supported by classically styled Doric columns on the two sides. Central doors might have a graceful border with typically rococo curves surrounding Gothic panels. The whole thing could well be supported by massive claw feet. The inevitable result was a coarse medley which could claim paternity in no particular style. The difference between these hodgepodges of the early Victorian era and those of the late Classical period, though, was an abiding romanticism. Overall, the lines were a little more rounded, the carving a little more fanciful, the designs simply more *feminine* than in previous years.

The dominant theme of artists and writers of the period was nature in all its glory, everywhere tinged with the soft-focus lens of romanticism. Where art and literature led, architecture and furniture followed. The result was Victoriana, and many purists consider the 1830s and 1840s to be the beginning of the end of good furniture design in this country.

The first Victorian furniture definable as such was the Gothic motif that flourished mainly from the 1830s through the 1850s. These vertical pieces of furniture were patterned after the soaring architecture of European cathedrals. The dominant motif was the pointed Gothic arch. It was worked into chair backs, secretary doors, whatnot fretwork, the pediments of frames and mirrors, headboards and footboards for beds, and the elaborate canopies that overhung many dressing tables. Furniture makers often combined an elongated arch with a roundel, a round, ornamental panel, to imitate the stained-glass windows of European medieval cathedrals.

The development and sophistication of furniture-making machinery about this time lowered the price of fashionable furniture to within the reach of most families. Until this time fine veneers had been expensive and available only in small sheets. However, by 1840 improved circular saws were capable of making exceptionally thin cuts on top-grade wood and in ever-larger pieces. As a result, furniture makers could cover entire tabletops with lovely quality wood veneers at a fraction of the price charged only a few years before.

Around 1850 an Ohio inventor perfected a bandsaw which could cut the most intricate designs in wood with, for that time, mind-boggling speed. The result was a nationwide flood of incredibly fanciful whatnots, sideboards, music stands, organs, mirror frames, and so forth, all overloaded with complex scrolls and intricate fretwork. Machines that carved wood almost as well as the human hand appeared shortly afterward. The virtues of fine hand-craftsmanship were soon overshadowed by a torrent of inexpensive machine-made furniture that adorned virtually every parlor, bedroom, and dining room in the land.

By the middle of the nineteenth century, romanticism was in full flower. Americans joyfully embraced the rococo period of Victoriana. This was the era best exemplified by the frequently fussy, pretentiously proud, but unquestionably ebullient years just before the Civil War. It was a time of fluid lines, lavish carving, and gay abandon in furniture design.

The Victorians developed an intense love of naturalism, and showed it by the profusion of floral and leaf motifs they attached to their furniture. Hundreds of thousands of dressers, commodes, and chests of drawers were built with wooden drawer pulls carved in the shape of leaves and fruit.

Homes had high ceilings during this time of growing affluence, and furniture makers took full advantage of the opportunity. They built massive wardrobes, sideboards, and bedsteads 8, 9, even 10 feet tall. Many of the beds were built with four turned posts and either a full or half tester, a fabric-covered framework supported by the posts. In the North the canopies were largely decorative. In the South they served the practical purpose of supporting the framework for a mosquito bar. Iron and brass beds came into vogue about this time, as did fancy wicker furniture and the dainty little twisted-iron ice cream chairs with their tiny round tables for two. Every fashionable home had a fainting couch in the parlor to cushion the frequent falls of those tightly corseted women, and a hall tree near the front door to receive umbrellas, coats, and the hats of the men of the house.

The small whatnot evolved into the more elaborate etagere, often embellished with a marble-topped lower shelf and a mirrored back panel. For the first time we see dressing bureaus with attached mirrors and small shelves to hold kerosene lamps or candlesticks.

Cabinetmakers heavily padded the backs of chairs and sofas for elegance and comfort. They then lavished the wooden framework of the chair or sofa with deeply carved roses, lilies, grapes, leaves, and open scrollwork. The typical fine sofa of the period had three humps to its back. Sometimes the back would also be divided into three sections, each upholstered separately and bordered to match the upper rail. A favorite first cousin of the sofa and a Victorian innovation was the meridienne, which had the base and seat of a regular sofa but only one arm and a sweeping high back. Dining chairs were usually built without upholstery on the backs, perhaps to discourage slouching at the table.

The cabriole leg was revived with enthusiasm by the Victorians and soon reached its most ornate form. It became so exaggerated on some small tables that the upper curve bowed out a full 6 or 7 inches before doubling back. These elaborate table legs were often adorned with garlands of carved fruit and vegetables, wooden ribbons and swags, and delicately molded feminine heads.

Faced with these excesses, it was predictable that public taste would soon rebel and begin looking for fresh ideas in furniture design. Charles Locke Eastlake, an English architect, stepped in to fill the need. In 1868 he published a book titled *Hints on Household Taste in Furniture, Upholstery and Other Details,* calling for a return to simpler, more geometric designs. He stressed quality construction and strong materials, an almost architectural approach to building furniture. Eastlake, like his contemporary, William Morris, was thoroughly revulsed by the morass of bad taste that filled homes on both sides of the Atlantic. Fashionable English men and women ignored him and his book, but Americans, always ready for something new, were fascinated by Eastlake's philosophy. The book was published in this country in 1872 and had an immediate, if shortlived, impact on American furniture design.

Eastlake's furniture was far more formal and restrained than that coming from his exuberant contemporaries. His designs had a distinctly rural, almost utilitarian ambiance, quite in contrast to the elaborate romanticism that engulfed others. He advocated squared-off corners and flat surfaces. Gone were undulating curves in favor of angles and geometric forms. Legs and supports became straight again, though often interrupted with bulbous details. He and those who followed his call used many ceramic tile inserts on hall trees and wash stands. Mirror and picture frames carried through with the geometric motifs, but like many of the sideboards of the period, they had well-proportioned finials on the pediments. Cabinetmakers frequently worked a simple spoon-shaped carving into the overall design.

Most Eastlake-style furniture was constructed of oak, though occasionally we find a piece in walnut. This isn't surprising. Oak is one of the sturdiest, if not the most elegant, of cabinet woods, and quite in keeping with Eastlake's thesis.

The vogue for Eastlake furniture lasted little more than a decade, but it presaged a change to come in American tastes.

Following on the heels of the romantic early Victorians and the austere Eastlake school, the furniture of the 1880s and 1890s is difficult to place into any category. A conglomeration of styles suddenly became fashionable again, Directoire, early Empire, Chinese—and added to these were a few new crazes. Individually, some of this late Victorian furniture wasn't too bad, and some was terrible. As a whole, it showed the poorest taste in all of America's furniture history.

For all of its problems and excesses, the Industrial Revolution did have some positive qualities. And one of these was that many more people had a great deal more discretionary income. However, some Americans were becoming wealthy with astonishing speed, and it seems they couldn't spend their money fast enough. They built massive mansions along the Hudson River in New York, on Chicago's Lake Shore Drive, and on the millionaire's playground, Jekyll Island in Georgia. And every burgeoning millionaire (or potential one) wanted his or her home to be more opulent than the one next door. They hired architects and interior designers and turned them loose with virtually unlimited expense accounts. The results, which all of America tried to follow, could only be described as gaudy.

Following the lead of English architect Norman Shaw, the architects abandoned interior doors on the ground floors of their clients' homes. In their place, they opened sweeping arches between rooms, then embellished these arches with every device at their command. Some of these openings between parlor and library or dining room and parlor were draped with swags of heavy brocade and velvet, silken tassels and ropes. Some had elaborate carved cornices and pediments that soared to reach the 12- and 14-foot-high ceilings. Other arches were subdivided into smaller, usually Moorish-style arches and pillars. A few managed to combine all this into one.

The craze for things Moorish permeated much of America during the latter part of the nineteenth century. Most of it was confined to architectural decor, though. About the only innovation as far as furniture was concerned was the ottoman. This was a round, deeply tufted, armless seat usually placed in the center of a room.

Otherwise, homeowners tended to fill their homes with ornate antiques from other periods in a quite eclectic fashion. In keeping with the vogue of the time for collecting and displaying art and bric-a-brac, we find many fancy wall shelves, small tables, whatnots, and bookcases. Wicker furniture, originally used as summer furniture on open porches, gained much popularity in response to a growing trend toward lightness and openness in new homes. Following the same movement, and echoing the Victorians' love of things oriental, they began to buy furniture with a delicate bamboo motif. Both the wicker and the bamboo fitted well with the new idea of bringing more light into a home. It was also about this time that people began to toy with the concept of bringing nature itself indoors. So, every fashionable home had at least one large potted Boston fern and a snake-like sansevieria or two. These plants were usually tucked into corners in hallways or parlors on fern stands, rather spindly tables some 3 feet high and with a top seldom larger than 18 inches square. These tables were made round, square, and octagonal, sometimes with marble tops, and usually with a shelf some 12 inches off the floor.

The rolltop desk was a feature of every professional's office, along with at least one bank of glass-fronted stacked bookcases. Metal furniture, including tons of brass and iron beds, abounded. An English firm introduced the enormously popular Morris chair to America just before the 1890s. A forerunner to our modern reclining lounger, it offered an adjustable back, the ultimate in comfort for that time.

As the century drew to a close, furniture makers began using more and more oak. It was almost universal for the ubiquitous round dining table and the pattern-backed, armless chairs that served in every kitchen and dining room. Almost none of these chairs were upholstered, most having solid, shaped seats or small caned sections.

We now arrive at a milestone in both political and furniture history. The Victorian era ended as Edward VII ascended the throne of England in 1901. The entire English-speaking world figuratively threw open the windows, took a deep breath, and heralded the dawn, not only of a new century, but of a new way of life. Out went the stuffy proprieties of Queen Victoria and in came a freshness and freedom of thought unlike any the world had ever known.

❀ 3 ❀

THE NEW ANTIQUES

The term "new antique" may seem to be an anomaly. It is, though, a phrase you'll hear frequently as you become more knowledge-able about antiques. It denotes quality furniture built from shortly before 1900 to approximately 1925. Not yet a hundred years old, so not legally classified as antiques, much of this furniture is, nev-ertheless, quite charming and a joy to collect and own.

A great deal happened in this country between 1895 and the years following the end of World War I. A few holdovers from the Victorian era existed, of course, but changes came, and they came fast. On both sides of the Atlantic men and women threw off the somberness of the previous century and began to hunger for all things new.

The stereoscope that graced every Victorian parlor gave way to moving pictures at the local vaudeville house. Americans happily replaced gas lighting with Mr. Edison's new invention. The tele-phone soon made hand-carried messages a thing of the past. Mil-lions of privies were joyfully abandoned as indoor plumbing be-came a practical reality for American homes.

Old mores broke down and great fortunes were made almost overnight. The new century spawned a generation of young men and women who were bright, restless, and grasping for the new and untried in their lives. Designers, most of whom were thor-oughly sick of the gaudy, ornate, overworked and overstuffed furniture of the late Victorian era, were only too happy to assuage their customers' clamor for simplicity.

Their philosophy was partly instigated, and greatly accelerated, by the arts and crafts movement which flourished in England during the 1890s. This movement protested the social, moral, and cultural turbulence that resulted from the Industrial Revolution. It opposed the imitative and often shoddy workmanship of the morass of factory-made furniture that was flooding the market. The leaders of the arts and crafts movement called for a return to hand-craftsmanship and quality construction. The movement was short-lived, partially because most people simply could not afford to buy handcrafted furniture and accessories in the age of machinery. The movement left its mark, though, by finally putting an end to the fussiness and pretentiousness of late Victorian stylings. Such straightforward materials as bamboo, wicker, and bentwood became popular as designers smoothed out lines and eliminated the fanciful, frilly "gingerbread" motifs so loved by carpenters and architects during the last decade of the nineteenth century.

Most of the furniture built during these thirty-five years or so could be classed as one of three styles: Art Nouveau, Mission Oak, or Art Deco. Technically "collectables," these are the antiques of the future. Many shops carry a large stock of these new antiques, and the dealers buy and sell them daily for a tidy profit. The prices on these pieces are, naturally, much more affordable than those on legitimate antiques. So, many of the most avid buyers are young people with an eye for quality but with very little discretionary cash.

Another large and growing segment of the new-antiques buying public are those just learning about the field. Either they don't have the money to invest large sums in antiques, or they wisely want to test the market with small investments before moving on to substantial purchases of more expensive pieces.

Regardless, absolutely no reason exists for *not* starting out with a few good pieces of furniture from one of the periods described in this chapter. You can always sell them or trade up later on to make room for more valuable furniture. Too, with each passing year these new antiques come closer to becoming legal antiques, and thus more valuable as an investment. The law of supply and demand inevitably will come into effect as more and more people become collectors. The prices of all antiques, traditional and "new," are thus bound to escalate in years to come.

Don't dismiss this period in American furniture just because the styles don't rate very high with collectors of more expensive antiques. Many a novice antique buff has furnished a house or apartment with a delightful and lighthearted eclectic mix of new antiques. The effect can be charming. These really are the *fun* antiques!

ART NOUVEAU (Approximately 1895–1920)

The Art Nouveau movement was not especially good or lasting. It was important in American furniture history, however, because it heralded the end of the dismal darkness that was the close of the Victorian era. Rebelling against the overembellished furniture that flooded the furniture marketplace of the late 1890s, some European designers developed new ideas, new concepts, that found immediate approval throughout the civilized world. They took a 180-degree turn from gingerbread and started designing furniture and accessories with simple, flowing, fluid lines. They took their cues from nature with its motion, curves, and endless cycling. Fairy-like tendrils wove in, out, and around the leaves and stems of flowers, fruit, and nuts. Foaming ocean waves broke over nude women, and graceful tree branches swept the earth. The entire effect was one of delicate sensuality and naturalness, with faint overtones of sentimental decadence.

The Art Nouveau years found their greatest expression in accessories, not furniture. This was the era that fostered the whirlwind careers of Louis Comfort Tiffany and others who worked in glass, china, pottery, and metal. Those substances were far easier to shape into the undulating styles of the time than was wood. Most wooden furniture during this period was custom-made, and therefore usually of good quality and fine woods. It is a real find to uncover a piece or two. Look for asymmetrical lines, stylized animal forms, and those slender nude or seminude women with their inviting upstretched arms and long flowing hair.

Far more available than wooden pieces are the popular floor lamps made of cast iron and brass. Refinished, they're a useful addition to any home and are always in demand in antique shops.

MISSION OAK (Approximately 1900–1920)

This sturdy, completely utilitarian, almost peasant style of furniture was a direct outgrowth of the arts and crafts movement. The style was an attempt to emulate the simple and functional furniture used by Spanish priests in mission churches.

The designers who worked in Mission Oak used only thick planks of solid oak, a common, exceptionally durable cabinet wood. They worked with the simplest construction methods, anchoring joints together, squared end against squared end, and fastened with substantial screws, pegs, and glue. You will seldom find more sophisticated joining methods such as mitering and dovetailing on Mission Oak furniture.

All Mission Oak has a squared-off, geometric feel. You will seldom see curved lines or fancy carvings on this style, but we do often find square or rectangular designs cut into the end panels of desks and library tables. Occasionally there will be a simple geometric design glued to the front of a case piece. In most instances, the original finish was a medium to dark natural wood tone. Mission Oak was almost never painted.

Sturdy leather, usually cowhide, was used frequently to upholster furniture with Mission Oak styling. If not leather, the upholstery was often an open-weave homespun fabric reminiscent of the rough cloth worn by monks in early California missions.

While Mission Oak was usually plain to the point of being quite ordinary, an occasional piece did show the hand of an exceptional designer. A Mission Oak sideboard with truly handsome brass strap hardware sold recently at auction for some $3000. This is unusual though. Most furniture from this period can be picked up for a tiny fraction of that sum.

Mission Oak had its virtues, certainly, but beauty was not often

This Mission Oak rocking chair shows transitional styling,
indicated by the curving lines on its back.

one of them. What it lacked in gracefulness, it made up for in
durability. It is extremely difficult to wear out or break furniture
made of thick oak planks! As tastes changed, many people became
bored with their solid and stolid Mission Oak but could hardly
discard furniture with generations of use left in it. So millions of
out-of-style pieces of Mission Oak furniture were relegated to rec-
reation rooms and summer cottages.

The resurgence of interest in Mission Oak today is causing us to
see it with renewed appreciation. And those three-cushion couches,
deep lounge chairs, library tables, and revolving four-sided bookcases are now finding their way into the antiques market.

ART DECO *(Approximately 1920–1935)*

Like Art Nouveau and Mission Oak, Art Deco was a minor and relatively undistinguished period in American furniture history. The Roaring Twenties followed right on the heels of World War I, causing a rapid and disturbing social turbulence in the United States. The Depression brought a temporary hiatus to most creative thought among our artists and designers. As a result Art Deco never developed the character and personality of most periods. It was lighthearted, useful, and quite practical, though. Even more

The iron and brass bridge lamp on the left is from the Art Deco period. The iron lamp on the right shows the more undulating lines of the Art Nouveau period.

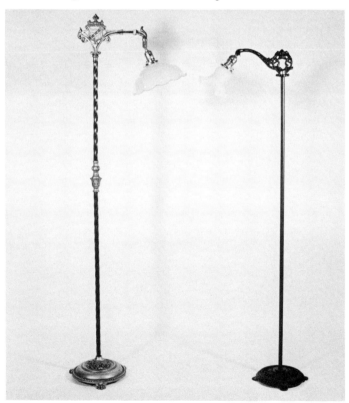

important, historically, is that Art Deco opened the door to "modern" furniture design by popularizing simple, geometric designs. We find many oval and octagonal parts, many angles and straight lines in Art Deco furniture. Functionality was the name of the game (inspired by the revolutionary ideas of Frank Lloyd Wright), so most furniture made during this period has little applied ornamentation.

Perhaps the most definitive quality of Art Deco was its effort to brighten up the home through use of clear primary colors. Many a breakfast table and matching set of chairs appeared painted in brilliant yellow, blue, red, green, or white. Often the chairs would boast one of the few fanciful trims of the period—painted floral decorations.

Little quality furniture was made during this time. Ordinary woods and ordinary lines were the rule rather than the exception.

4

How Do You Know It's Old?

Rarely will anyone offer you a *fake* antique. A fake is quite different from a reproduction. The fake antique is a deliberate attempt to deceive the customer by artificially aging and distressing wood to simulate the effects of wear, and then passing the item off as genuine.

Only a great deal of skill and effort by an experienced and devious cabinetmaker can pull off this chicanery faced with close scrutiny of the object by a knowledgeable person. Because of the costs involved in antique forgeries, this faking is practiced only on pieces that command exceptionally high prices. No reputable cabinetmaker would be involved in such deception.

Every once in a while today you will read of a con concerning a dressing table reputedly from Marie Antoinette's bedroom or an inlaid desk supposedly used by Napoleon on Elba. When the whole truth comes out, the "antique" was actually constructed in a back room workshop somewhere three weeks before being offered for sale with a five-figure price tag. Such goings-on are rare, and most of us will never encounter such a problem. Reproductions are another story.

Reproductions, in contrast to fakes, are honestly sold as new furniture built in the style of another era. People have admired antiques for many, many years, both for their beauty and as an investment. The coming of the age of machinery made it practical to duplicate earlier furniture styles at reasonable prices. The vogue seems to have gained momentum in the United States in the late 1800s and continues today. Reproductions abound, with virtually every furniture style available to today's consumers. Any large furniture store will have Duncan Phyfe dining room sets, Early American living room sets, and Queen Anne bedroom furniture. The best of these reproductions are excellent, but they do not have the monetary value of genuine antiques.

As a collector you must learn to tell these reproductions from the genuine pieces. Many times a piece of furniture is made in the style of another day and sold quite honestly as a reproduction. It then passes from one owner to another, is sold over and over, and garners a few nicks and a full coat of grime along the way. Within a few years all knowledge of its origins is long lost. The last person to own it may quite honestly believe it to be an antique and offer to sell it as such. Yet, as a reproduction, it is still just used furniture.

How *do* you separate used furniture from the genuine article?

Your first step is to recognize furniture styles of the past. You must learn to spot the one or two "hopefuls" in a roomful of junk. Just being able to recognize the type of leg and foot that Chippendale used isn't enough. The lovely old chair you unearth in the dusty back room of a secondhand store may indeed have those legs and feet and it just might be a genuine Chippendale. It is far more likely, however, that it will be a *reproduction* of the original Chippendale, a piece of furniture built within the past few years.

You can tell the reproduction from the genuine by a series of tests and observations you'll learn here. They'll help you avoid the costly mistake of buying secondhand furniture when you think you're buying antiques.

Almost every serious collector and dealer is fooled some time in his or her career, though. Certainly it has happened to me. My most glaring mistake was a beautiful rocking chair. I found it at an estate auction conducted on the lawn of a home in my town. This chair was the only "antique" at the sale, was in fine condition, and was quite typical of the romantic styles of around 1870 or so. My preauction examination showed that previous owners had worn out at least two seats. The chair had been made to hold a round leather seat. Nail holes within the seat channel showed me that one had indeed been there at some time. A series of nail holes on the upper surface of the wooden part of the seat indicated that the original leather seat had worn out and another larger one had been tacked in place. This was a common practice, and I find that many, many antique chairs are in this condition. That replacement seat, too, had obviously worn out. It was gone and someone had nailed a piece of plywood on the underside of the wooden seat, then covered the hole with a foam-filled cushion. Those worn-out seats plus the authentic design convinced me the chair was, indeed, an antique.

The chair was painted a bright red, and foolishly, I didn't check beneath that paint. Once the chair had been stripped I discovered two corrugated fasteners had been used for reinforcement on the underside of the seat, and they certainly appeared to have been put in during the original construction. That was my first indication something was wrong, since corrugated fasteners are a fairly recent innovation.

Some of the glue holding the stretchers in the legs had dissolved during stripping, and that gave me my second clue. I saw the previously hidden wood at the ends of the stretchers was far too light to be over a hundred years old. As described later in this chapter, all wood darkens with age, even that which has not been subjected to wear, grime, furniture polish, and air pollutants.

My conclusion was that I had actually bought a reproduction, probably one made during the 1920s or 1930s. This episode taught me an important lesson I'll pass on to you. Be wary if you go to an auction or estate sale and find only one "antique" in the lot. Most people who love beautiful antique furniture will own more than one piece. So, if their households are put up for auction, the offering will contain several pieces of antique furniture.

On the other side of the coin, don't take it for granted that *every* piece of furniture at an *antique* sale is really old. Sometimes a reproduction or two will be slipped in among the genuine antiques. Detection can be difficult if *all* the furniture at the sale is dusty and many pieces need repair (as often happens at estate sales and country auctions.)

Your best defense against the costly mistake of buying reproductions is to become knowledgeable about the ways furniture was made. Be aware of the ways wood ages and furniture wears. Learn to recognize the ways wood was cut years ago and the old ways of joining different parts of furniture. Learn what old screws and nails look like. All this, plus the ability to recognize authentic styles, will help you know whether that Victorian table you discover in a secondhand store in Atlanta was made in 1865 or 1965.

I suggest you also develop a healthy skepticism when buying from people you don't know. Just don't believe every story you hear that starts off, "This belonged to my great-grandmother...."

In contrast to many other substances, wood undergoes marked changes as it ages. It shrinks. It darkens. It shows the effects of daily use. It acquires a soft patina that can't be duplicated by any modern finishing method. These are some of the reasons antique furniture has so much character and is so beautiful. They also can be some of your primary aids in determining the age of a piece of furniture.

SHRINKAGE

All live, growing wood contains natural moisture. Once the tree is cut, though, the moisture begins to dry up. Properly cured wood will retain most of its finished size and shape, but inevitably some shrinkage will occur through the years as natural moisture continues to evaporate. The hardwoods (cherry, rosewood, teak, mahogany, maple, ash, oak, walnut) will shrink less than the softwoods (pine, poplar, spruce). So any of the distortions or problems mentioned in this section will usually be more acute with softwoods than with the hard varieties, assuming the woods are the same age.

Most of the shrinkage in wood takes place across the grain. Very little occurs with the grain (lengthwise of the tree). This peculiarity of nature causes many little problems in old furniture.

Frequently you will find framed panels of wood which have split, resulting in a crack ¼ inch or more wide. These cracked pan-

The enclosed panel in this oak commode has split from natural shrinkage of the wood, a common occurrence in antique furniture.

els are found in desks, commodes, dressers—any case piece where the cabinetmaker set a fairly thin panel of wood into grooves of a thicker wooden frame. The really astute fellows knew what was likely to happen with time and just inserted the panels loose. That way, the thin wood was able to shrink and pull in without splitting. As a rule, any panel which shrank without splitting will be a little lighter at one or both of its side edges. This is because those edges have been exposed to the air a shorter time than the main part of the panel.

Some cabinetmakers insisted on glueing or nailing the panels in place, perhaps thinking they were doing a better job. In time that wood began to dry out. Something had to give as the wood shrank, and inevitably, the thin panels could not compete with glue and hardware. They split from the tension.

Drawer bottoms and the backboards of some case pieces were nearly always made of thin, soft pine boards, so they shrank more than the hardwood from which the body of the piece was made. Many of the dressers, chests of drawers, and desks I find suffer from this problem. The drawer bottoms are split or pulled out of the shallow grooves of the side or back of the drawer (depending upon which way the grain of the wood in the drawer bottom lies). Backboards were nearly always nailed to the body of the piece, so they split even though the dresser, chest, or desk itself remained quite sturdy and solid.

Some furniture will even shrink out of shape in time. This is most noticeable on round tabletops which become slightly oval as the boards contract from side to side. You can be pretty sure, then, that a pine table is old if the top is an inch or so out of round.

Every once in a while you'll find an antique which was put together with wooden pegs. If the piece is very old, those pegs may be protruding a fraction of an inch beyond the surface of the table apron, chair, or whatever. This is because the pegs were whittled lengthwise of the grain of very hard wood and shrank little. Yet the body of the piece of furniture shrank noticeably *across* the grain, allowing the pegs to project in time.

TOOL MARKS

Rub your fingers along the underside of an antique tabletop and along the backboard of an old case piece. You'll find that those old craftsmen (who had to do all the finishing work by hand) seldom wasted much energy planing *unexposed* surfaces of wood. Only the very finest and most expensive pieces got the royal treatment of having back and undersides as smooth and well-finished as the tops and fronts.

Usually this rough, unexposed wood will still bear saw marks. And those saw marks can give you a good indication of the ap-

This tabletop was made from straight-cut lumber.

proximate age of the piece. Any piece of furniture constructed before about 1830 will have been made of wood cut and sawed by hand. The resulting saw marks on those rough surfaces are straight and usually quite irregular. Around 1830 the age of machinery made possible power-driven sawmills which still used straight blades and which made relatively smooth but still straight cutting marks on the wood. Around 1850 sawmills began using buzz saws which left clearly definable circular cutting marks on wood. So if you're debating about the age of an antique just hold the rough, unplaned surfaces up to a strong light and let it shine across the item at an angle. You should be able to see quite easily whether or not the piece was sawed by hand, by straight saw, or by circular saw.

Even the *planed* exposed surfaces of wood in old furniture will not usually be as even as that in new furniture. For one thing, antique furniture predates electric-belt sanders which can remove surface irregularities in wood in minutes. Run your fingers lightly over the surface of an old table, for instance, and you'll be able to feel those slight valleys and hills typical of antique furniture.

CUT OF THE WOOD

Be aware, too, of the width of the boards when inspecting an antique. Some old tabletops have boards 18 to 20 inches wide, much wider than any cabinet wood used today. Also, those furniture makers a few generations ago frequently used random widths of lumber in constructing a tabletop or desk. Modern furniture makers usually use boards of identical width, unless they're trying to emulate an old style. The lumber used in antique furniture was also heavier than that used today. A few generations ago furniture makers were concerned not only with turning out a beautiful product but also with making one that would stand up to hard use. These are two of the main reasons antique furniture is still lovely and usable after so many years of wear.

Notice the difference in the grain of this quarter-sawn oak tabletop. The characteristic wavy grain is quite distinctive and easy to spot.

Many antiques made of oak during the nineteenth century were constructed of quarter-sawn wood. Quarter-sawing is a method of cutting wood in which the log is sectioned into quarters before being cut into boards. The result is a quite distinctive wavy grain. The pattern looks much like the ripples on a pond. This fashionable style wasted a lot of wood and soon went out of vogue.

PATINA

Patina is that much-prized glow wood acquires after many years of handling, polishing, and just plain aging. I have a friend who had never given much thought to antique furniture. My enthusiasm for antiques, however, started her thinking in that direction, even though she knew absolutely nothing about the relative qualities of antique and modern furniture. She looked at some good reproductions in the best local furniture store, then came by my house to look at my collection. Her first comment after examining a dining chair was, "You can see so much deeper into this wood than in that at the store." What she was seeing was the patina, the natural depth and color of antique furniture which no artificial process can duplicate on new wood.

The best way to learn to recognize this natural patina is to place an old, well-cared-for piece of furniture (which has never been stripped) next to a new piece of a comparable color and wood. The difference will be obvious, just as it was for my friend.

Assuming an antique is constructed of one type of wood and is not a mixture of several, it should exhibit the same patina on all exposed finished surfaces. Be suspicious if you find an antique where one section of wood is markedly different from the rest. That section could be a recent repair or replacement. Such an alteration would substantially reduce the value of the piece.

The above caution goes double for applied trims. Some unscrupulous people will try to upgrade a fairly common and plain antique by glueing on fancy trims to simulate a more expensive one. These additions can include entire borders of pressed or carved trim on a table or china cabinet. Other alterations could be fancy wooden motifs on the back of a plain rocking chair or the fronts of dresser drawers.

The people who vandalize a good antique this way are not only dishonest but usually foolish as well. Quite often a simple primitive antique (that is, one of plain design, made long ago with local materials and hand tools) is far more valuable than a later style complete with factory-made decorations.

These additions aren't hard to spot. The wood will lack the patina of the piece of furniture to which they're applied. Often they will be lighter in color, or may look "new" in comparison to the rest of the piece. Check the edges of the trim—where it joins the drawer front or whatever. If the trim is firmly affixed on an antique you will see a slight buildup of old varnish and wax (even dirt) at the joining. If the trim is loose, pry it out a bit and peer at the wood underneath. The trim's design should be clearly evident there. If the color and patina of the wood extends unbroken around and under the trim, however, you can be quite sure the decoration was applied recently. Old wood which has been exposed to the air acquires a different patina than that which has been protected, as under a trim which was applied at the time the piece of furniture was constructed.

Unfinished but exposed wood, such as on the backs of chests of drawers, usually becomes much darker than the finished wood on the front of the piece. You will learn to recognize the characteristic tone of old, unvarnished wood in time. Coupled with a deep patina on the finished wood, it is a good indication of an authentic antique.

If you are at all suspicious about the age of a piece of furniture, try to check the condition of any completely unexposed and unfinished wood in the piece. For instance, check the ends of chair stretchers, the part which is inserted a half inch or so into the chair leg. Although unexposed, this wood would have darkened on a genuine antique. On relatively new furniture this unexposed wood will still look fresh and new. The stain or finish applied to the exposed surfaces of the wood of new furniture usually does not penetrate into those joints.

Another test for authenticity is to scratch the finish of a piece of furniture in some concealed spot. On new furniture the color will extend just under the surface, with light-colored wood under the stain. On old furniture the wood will be dark all the way through from natural aging.

NORMAL WEAR

Only furniture which is never used survives without nicks and scratches. Look for worn edges, cuts, stains in the wood, and any other evidence of everyday wear and tear. Hardwoods will show less wear and tear than softwoods. You can do a little test to demonstrate the relative "wearability" of one wood over another. Place a scrap of a hardwood such as walnut or oak next to a scrap of a softwood such as pine or poplar. Hit each with a hammer, using about the same amount of force. The blow will have little effect on the hardwood but will make a major dent in the softwood. This should prove to you quite graphically that a softwood table should show a great deal of wear if it is a genuine antique, while a hardwood table would show proportionately less wear.

When examining a piece of furniture, ask yourself, "How would I use this?" Pick it up or sit on it or open the drawers or place an object on it. Multiply any action you took by a lifetime of use and you will know where that piece of furniture would show normal wear.

The front stretchers of chairs sometimes will be worn down on top from generations of people resting their feet there. The back edge of the two rear legs may be worn from those same people leaning back on the chair. On very old chairs the finials that decorate the top of the back posts may be slightly worn. They may even be dark and greasy-looking from years of use. A series of concentric nail holes in a wooden seat shows that several wood, fiber, or leather seats postdated the original leather or cane when it wore out.

Often you'll find ink stains on office furniture, a lasting memento of the days before ball-point pens came into being. The underside of the front edge of kneehole desks will sometimes be worn. The front inside corners of those kneehole desks are nearly always scarred from people pushing chairs in and out.

Knobs and handles and the areas around them often show undeniable signs of age and use. Many case pieces such as pie safes and secretaries, especially if made of softwood, will have distinct gouges around the knobs (usually on the right side) where generations of fingernails collided with the wood. These knobs, if made of wood, will almost always have a characteristic dark, greasy look.

Even metal hardware can leave signs of age on old wood. Brass will tarnish, of course, but this usually leaves no lasting marks on the wood it touches. This is *not* the case with some of the cheaper hardware manufactured a while back. I once spent a couple of frustrating hours trying to get rid of the deep black marks on a dresser left by some miserable copperplated hardware. The drawer pulls were at least a hundred years old and for ninety-nine of those years they evidently have been merrily corroding away, leaving a deeper and deeper imprint of their pattern in the wood. (I finally got most of the marks out with sandpaper and bleach and replaced the old pulls with some antique brass ones of almost the same shape.)

Many times you'll find antiques whose hardware has been replaced at least once. Sometimes the evidence is not black marks but plugged up holes that indicate where the original bolts went through the wood. You'll usually see these old holes most easily from the inside of drawers because the replacement hardware was not the same width as the original and new holes were drilled to accommodate it.

These holes are no problem, they only indicate that the hardware is not the original issue. While that may detract a bit from the value of the antique, it is so common that no one worries about it. In fact, if replacement hardware itself is very old, it just shows that the antique is far older.

Drawers are a good indication of age in an antique. The sides and bottoms of most old drawers were made of a softwood, usually pine, and it wore quickly. You can look for three signs of age on softwood drawers. First, the bottoms should be worn quite smooth. Second, the tops of the sides may be worn down a little at the very back of the drawer. Third, the bottoms of the sides may be worn concave at the very front of the drawer. These last two items are the result of the drawer being tilted forward as it was opened. This common type of wear is the reason so many old dresser drawers drop down a little when pulled out.

JOININGS

Your most obvious clue to the approximate date of an antique may be the way it was put together. Always check the edges of drawers. On most furniture styles the hardwood front will be joined to the softwood sides with some sort of dovetail joint, except for some primitives and Mission Oak which used butt joints. Most dovetail joints look very much alike—a series of alternating and interlocking wedge-shaped joints. Early cabinetmakers cut them by hand and often made the "tails" an inch or more wide. These old handmade dovetails are relatively crude and uneven, too. By the mid-nineteenth century, furniture makers were using machine-cut

The extremely crude hand-cut dovetails on the small drawer on the left indicate this drawer was probably made before the mid-nineteenth century. The center drawer shows the even, rounded dovetails typical of the mid-Victorian years. The drawer on the right came from a cabinet made around 1890 and shows the more even spacing and cut of recent dovetails.

dovetails. The first machine-cut dovetails were smaller and more uniform than the old hand-cut ones, and were often round rather than wedge-shaped. By around 1880 most dovetail joints were very similar to the wedge-shaped joints in use today.

Early cabinetmakers frequently used pinned mortise and tenon joints for tables and chairs. The basic part of this joint was identical to modern mortise and tenon joints. Then, as now, a thin slot was cut into one half of the joint (the outside edge of a bed footboard, for instance) and a projection to fit the slot was cut into the other half of the joint (the upper edge of the leg). These craftsmen went one step further, though, by drilling a small hole through the finished joint and inserting a wooden pin for added reinforcement.

Wooden pegs were used often in furniture construction a few generations back, not always because nails weren't available, but because hardwood dowels made stronger joints. Before the advent of power-driven machinery these pegs were whittled by hand. Therefore any piece of furniture with irregular wooden pegs can be dated before about 1840. After that date furniture makers used machine-made dowels which were about as cylindrical as the ones in use today.

HARDWARE

You can't always judge an antique's age by the type of nail or screw used in its construction, simply because it is too easy to replace hardware. A very old piece could have modern screws because someone recently reinforced a weak joint, for instance. On the other hand, a forger could use very old salvaged hardware on a cleverly made fake.

Assuming the hardware on an antique is the original, though, you have some guidelines to help you. Until about the end of the eighteenth century, cabinetmakers used hand-forged nails. Around 1790, though, nails stamped out of sheet iron with blunt ends but hand-forged heads became available. Some twenty years later blacksmiths began producing the entire nail by stamping. And by 1850 cabinetmakers were using wire nails with round heads and sharp points, quite similar to those we use today.

The very earliest screws were wide, crude, and had irregular threads cut by hand with a file. Slots in the heads were likely to be off center, since they were cut with a hand-held hacksaw. Around 1800 machinists developed efficient screw-making machinery, and from that point on we see screws fairly similar to those in use today.

Handmade hinges on very old primitive antiques will usually be made of crude, uneven sheets of iron. The screw holes will often be irregularly placed.

LABELS AND OTHER IDENTIFYING FACTORS

An authentic pasted-on manufacturer's label always adds to the value of an antique. If the label is dated, you also have incontrovertible proof of the piece's age. You'll find the labels on dressers most often in a drawer, pasted to the upper side of one of the drawer bottoms. Look for the label on an old desk on the back of the small door that separates the bank of pigeonholes. On tables the label will be on the underside of the tabletop, and on chairs it will be on the underside of the chair seat.

One of my daughters once bought a lovely old mahogany dental cabinet at an estate auction. It turned out to have a complete finishing record on a label pasted to the bottom of one of the drawers. The label listed eleven finishing steps, including staining, filling, two coats of varnish with sanding in between each, rubbing, and the final inspection. Beside each step was the finisher's code number and the date he worked on the cabinet. The record covers a five-week period from November 6, 1917, until December 12 of the same year. This unusual cabinet with its twenty-two shallow drawers, glass-fronted sterilizer compartments, beveled mirror, and beautifully paneled back is not a "legal" antique yet. It will be within a very few years, however, and that label will add a great deal to its value then.

Any old label may be quite brittle and its glue completely dried out. One in this condition is easily lost, but you certainly want to preserve it to verify the age of your antique. I suggest one simple but effective method. Gently push some all-purpose glue under the label with a cotton swab or small brush. Press the label down and allow it to dry. Brush on a coat or two of satin-finish polyurethane varnish to protect the paper from further deterioration. If the label is in good condition, just cover it with a sturdy piece of clear plastic film. Then securely tape the edges of the film.

Although I've never seen one, I've read that another form of "label" was used during the late eighteenth and early nineteenth centuries. It seems that some manufacturers of Windsor chairs *branded* the undersides of chair seats with their names. Such a chair would be quite unusual and therefore even more valuable than an unbranded chair. I guess those early chair makers were proud of their work and branded it to be sure everyone knew who the producer was. Chair makers sometimes branded a Windsor chair with the name of the buyer, too. This "label" probably served to identify ownership in case of theft, much as we engrave our social security numbers on television sets and cameras today.

Some of the most charming "labels" were never intended as such. Old newspapers can be just about as good as a manufacturer's label in setting the approximate date of an antique. Back before the advent of commercial shelf paper and relatively inexpensive wallpapers people frequently used old copies of the local newspaper to line shelves and trunks. Be extremely careful to preserve any such treasures you find pasted into an antique. Not only can they date the item, but the papers themselves are usually quite charming with their lovely old steel engravings, quaint type, and fascinating copy.

I once found an old British seaman's trunk which had been lined with a copy of the London *Illustrated Times.* The newspaper was in pretty bad condition but still intact enough that I could read some of the articles. In one I found a reference to that week's date—in October 1867. The trunk of heavy planks and crude handmade iron hardware obviously had been used for many years before it was lined with the newspaper by some British salt. So I had authenticated information for the approximate age of the trunk. I preserved the paper as described above, and ended up with a one-of-a-kind gem of an antique. And guess where I found this beauty. At a garage sale, no less. The family had been using it for a toy box for its little son. They only decided to sell it because he kept dropping the heavy lid on his fingers!

5

GENERAL REPAIR TECHNIQUES

All right. You've brought that rickety antique home from the garage sale and now you're ready to restore it from Early Secondhand to late Victorian. Before you grab your rubber-tipped hammer, though, you need to make a checklist of possible damage and problems. That way you'll be prepared with all the necessary materials, equipment, and parts at the time you need them. You'll also know exactly what you face in the way of repairs so you can take the steps in logical order.

1. Clean the piece thoroughly with paint thinner and/or a weak ammonia and water solution.
2. Remove all past Band-aid-like repairs, including nails, scrap wood braces, and baling wire tourniquets.
3. Test for loose joints.
4. Check the condition of the hardware.
5. Look for broken or missing parts.
6. Test the stability of the drawers and doors.
7. Look for warpage.
8. Test the level of the piece, determining if any problem stems from uneven legs or loose joints.
9. Look for evidence of dry rot on legs.
10. Check for any "glorification" with modern trim or decorations.
11. Look for loose, blistered, or cracked veneer.

With this information you'll know how much effort and time you'll have to expend to repair the monster. Take one word of advice, though. Certainly, you'll take care of any problem which threatens the stability of the piece or detracts from its inherent beauty. However, and this caveat applies to the finishing process, too, do not go too far. Remember, you want the final result of your work to look like a genuine antique which has seen years of loving use and care. You don't want a piece of furniture which could pass for a reproduction straight out of the show window of your local furniture store. Leave a few imperfections. Let your antiques retain the dignity of their years, of their own personalities. After all, isn't that why we love them?

Now, this chapter does not go into a great deal of detail about standard woodworking techniques. Every bookstore and library has many fine books devoted entirely to that subject for those who want basic instruction. It would be redundant for me to include that here. This chapter deals with the special problems encountered in renovating *antique* furniture.

With that in mind, let's start at the beginning.

GLUEING

You'll want your finished work to look as authentic as possible. Always use glue in preference to screws when securing a joint. A well-glued joint is far stronger than one joined only with screws, since metal tends to wear wood, especially at stress points. In time the joint will loosen, simply because the screw works loose. Old wood is often dry and brittle. You can easily split a delicate member by trying to joint it to another with a screw. This does not mean that you will *never* use metal fasteners in renovating your antiques. Many times you will combine glue and screws on hidden joints, just as the old craftsmen did when they first constructed the piece.

Early furniture makers used glue made from animal hide or fish products, which they heated to a liquid before each use. While a few purists today still contend this is the only way to get a good strong joint, I and most of the antique repair buffs I know, disagree. We get excellent results with the yellow wood glue available in most hardware stores. It requires no mixing, stays liquid in the bottle, dries fairly quickly, cleans up with water, and forms a strong, water-resistant bond when dry.

SHOULD I TAKE IT APART? One school of thought regarding antique renovation says a piece of furniture must be completely disassembled and every joint reglued. Frankly, I can't quite see this unless the antique is falling apart anyway. If any antique is still sturdy after generations of use, the chances are it will continue that way for a long time to come. You're only asking for a lot of extra work if you take apart joints that do *not* need repair or reglueing. My advice is to just work on the wobbly or damaged parts, and leave the solid ones alone.

When you *do* have to dismantle an antique, you should use either a rubber-tipped mallet or a regular hammer with the business end covered with a thick pad of rags. Tap gently at first, then with more force as the old glue begins to give way.

REMOVING HIDDEN HARDWARE Every once in a while I'll be dismantling an antique when I find the parts refuse to separate, even though I know the glue is broken. The answer usually hinges on a hidden nail or two buried inside the wood, its head right at or below the surface. Years before, the old glue lost its grip on life and some home-repair buff probably tried to shore up the wobbly legs or stabilize a top rail by *nailing* it together. (I have unpleasant thoughts about these people!) Once when taking a fragile little fern stand apart, I found an incredible thirty-seven tiny nails inflicted on the poor thing. It took me over an hour to dig them out of the slender legs.

Often you are not able to see the head of the nail, so you won't know where to dig. One solution is to try to force the two parts apart a bit until you can actually see a portion of the nail's shank. Use a hacksaw then to saw through the nail. If you can't get the entire hacksaw in, around, or under the nail, just take the blade out of the tool and use it alone. Once the parts are separated you can then use pliers to pull the nails out of the wood.

Another method of getting a buried nail out of wood is to drive it through. This works if the nail is very slender, has essentially no head, and the point lies close to the outside edge of the wood. You

Sometimes digging is the only way to remove nails which have been used to repair antique furniture.

rest the antique on a horizontal surface to brace it, then force the nail through with a nail set—the small tool used to pound nails below the surface of wood.

The last alternative is one that *always* works, but does cause considerable damage to the antique. You take a tool such as an awl and dig some wood away from, around, and under the nail's head. This gives you enough room to get a pair of needle-nosed pliers or a diagonal cutter in to pull the nail out. You will have to repair that hole with wood filler later on.

CODING IDENTICAL PARTS Be sure to mark any seemingly identical parts you remove from an antique, coding them so you'll know just where each should go upon reassembling. That way you won't be confused about which stretcher went on the top left and which on the bottom right. Surprisingly, even the matched spindles from the back of a chair are often of different lengths and the ends may have different diameters.

REMOVING OLD GLUE Once the necessary parts are disassembled, you need to sand away all the old dried glue. Fresh glue will *not* adhere over the old stuff. Old glue can be especially difficult to remove, too. Sometimes boiling vinegar will dissolve old glue. Or you can use coarse sandpaper on those sections which will be hidden once the antique is reassembled.

Often the hardest glue-removal job is trying to get the old glue out of sockets. I've found the easiest way is simply to drill it out with a drill bit of the same diameter as the hole.

GETTING STARTED Remember, don't try to glue fifteen different pieces back together in one operation. This is about as efficient as trying to paper the ceiling and four walls of a room at one time. Something will always be falling out or down while you're pushing something else in. Glue a few pieces at a time, clamp them, and allow the section to dry overnight before you tackle another section. Be sure to wipe off with a damp cloth any glue that oozes out of the joints. Once it is dry, wood glue is difficult to remove, and will quite effectively block your stain or oil from penetrating the wood.

Often the easiest way to clean old glue from a socket is to drill it out with an electric drill. Use a bit the same diameter as the socket and take care not to enlarge the hole.

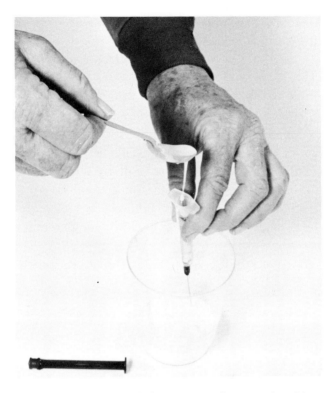

Mix one part water with three parts yellow woodworking glue and pour the mixture into a hypodermic syringe. The thinned glue will flow easily through the needle.

Periodically, throughout the reglueing of several parts of an antique, you should set the piece of furniture on a flat surface and check its level. Check both horizontal and vertical planes.

At times you may not need to take an antique apart for reglueing. Perhaps one leg of a chair, for instance, is just a trifle loose, but not really wobbling. The answer in that case is to force glue into the joint while the two parts are still in place. This method also works when you're faced with a narrow crack on a tabletop or solid wood seat, a crack too small to accept a glue-laden spatula. The most satisfactory tool for this operation is a hypodermic syringe filled with a diluted solution of glue and water. Yellow glue as it comes from the bottle is usually too thick to flow through the needle, so mix about one part water to three parts glue. You can buy inexpensive hypodermic syringes in drugstores in some areas and in many large building-supply stores. If you have trouble locating them, just ask some commercial furniture repairer where he or she gets a supply.

Insert the needle of the filled syringe deeply into the joint or crack and press the plunger. Don't skimp. Remember this glue is diluted, and besides much of it will probably run out of the joint while you're working. Wipe off any glue that drips onto the finished surface of the antique, then clamp overnight.

CLAMPING THE GLUED ANTIQUE   You can't do a good job of glueing wood without using clamps. Natural tension between parts, the

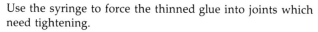

Use the syringe to force the thinned glue into joints which need tightening.

Inexpensive bungie cords are useful and versatile in the workshop.

weight of the antique, or just plain gravity can cause freshly glued joints to pull apart slightly, thereby substantially reducing the quality of the repair. To be effective, joined parts must be firmly butted together, and the glue must penetrate the pores of the wood. The only practical solution is to firmly clamp every glued joint immediately after joining the parts.

C clamps and pipe clamps are the old standbys in most workshops, and they're indispensable in repairing antiques. C clamps in two or three sizes will take care of the small jobs. Pipe clamps of 4 to 6 feet can help stabilize even large dressers, chests, or buffets. Pipe clamps are bought in two pieces. One piece is attached to the end of a section of lead pipe. This part of the clamp has a screw handle which moves the clamp along the pipe with each revolution. The other piece of the clamp has a locking mechanism. It is placed along the pipe and slides back and forth as needed. To clamp a 40-inch-wide cabinet, for instance, you would place the locking section at about 41 inches down the pipe. After glueing the cabinet, the assembled pipe clamp is placed along its length. The screw handle is tightened until the clamps are firmly grabbing the cabinet. One or two more revolutions and the clamps form an excellent vise to hold the cabinet while the glue dries.

A good selection of clamps can be quite expensive, and while you're building up a collection you can certainly use less expensive surrogate types. Plain cotton clothesline can be quite effective. Using a length of clothesline, pass it around the glued antique twice and tie the ends securely. Tighten it by placing a screwdriver or short length of dowel between the two lines and twisting them until the desired tension is reached. Secure the screwdriver or dowel behind some part of the furniture to hold the tension. Bungie cords are another inexpensive alternative to hardware clamps. Their end hooks and strong elastic cords make them ideal for irreg-

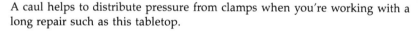

A caul helps to distribute pressure from clamps when you're working with a long repair such as this tabletop.

ularly shaped pieces. I use bungie cords regularly when clamping chair legs and spindles.

Even more unconventional "clamps" can be improvised for those hard-to-secure glueing jobs. Old inner tubes can be cut into gargantuan rubber bands that have endless possibilities. Spring-type clothespins are good for clamping edges and very small work. And you can use tape to hold sections of delicate trim in place while glue hardens.

Regardless of the type of clamp you use, though, be sure to place thin wood or rags between it and the wood to prevent damage at the point of contact. A thin strip of wood is known as a caul and is especially useful when glueing long edges such as tabletops or when clamping softwoods. Just be sure to place waxed paper between the caul and the wood to prevent excess glue from wedding the two together.

TIGHTENING SOCKETS

Some sockets in antiques wear too large to grip the companion piece, even when fresh glue is used. Don't ever bank on a thick layer of glue filling in gaps of ⅛ inch or so. It just won't happen. One way to increase the size of a spindle end, however, so it will fit a socket that is too large is to brush on a coat of glue, then wrap the end with thread or a few thicknesses of nylon stocking. This artificially enlarged end should fit the socket once it is given another coat of glue. Or coat the end of the spindle with glue, insert it into the socket, and then fill any remaining space with short pieces of glue-dipped wooden toothpicks.

A more professional (albeit more troublesome) way does exist to tighten sockets. Use a piece of hardwood dowel as long as the depth of the socket but a bit larger in diameter. Drill out the old socket with a drill bit the same diameter as the piece of new dowel. Glue the dowel into this new, enlarged socket and allow it to dry overnight. Then bore a new socket in the center of that dowel, using a bit the diameter of the old spindle's end. Insert the spindle, along with plenty of glue, into this new socket. Once the glue hardens, this type of joint has an exceptionally tight bond. It's the best method I know to reinforce worn sockets.

SPLIT AND CRACKED WOOD

As mentioned before old wood dries out as its natural moisture gradually lessens. Add to that the drying effects of our centrally heated homes and you have the catalyst for one of the most common problems in antique furniture—split wood. A split will often begin as just a hairline crack. At first it is barely noticeable. Bit by bit, though, it creeps along and gets deeper until finally the desk side panel, tabletop, or whatever, splits into two pieces. Sometimes a piece of wood, usually one under pressure, such as a chair seat, will develop a crack along the length of the wood, apparently spontaneously. Almost any split, though, regardless of its nature, can be repaired with glue and clamps. The sooner you catch it the better.

Cracks on large-surface pieces such as tabletops and chair seats are easy to repair. Just spread glue generously along both sides of the crack and clamp the two parts together. Place a level across the surface to make sure the pressure of the clamps has not bowed the parts out of line.

As described in Chapter 4, framed panels in old furniture often split because they were glued firmly into place when made. After years of natural shrinkage the panels cannot slide out of their channels and wood won't stretch, so they did the only thing possible. They split down the grain.

When faced with such a split panel first try to loosen the panel's pieces from the side channels. Slide a flexible spatula into the groove and try to work the glue loose. If you can manage this, the panel will slide freely. If you're successful, work some glue along both edges of the split and push the two pieces together. Wipe off the excess glue and hold the wood together with masking tape until the glue dries.

Many panels will not come loose that easily. Assuming the split panel is on a framed door, then, take the door off its hinges and disassemble the framework. This will free up the panel. Glue the

The thick boards which formed the seat of this office chair were separating when I found it. The arrows point to the resulting cracks. A former owner had tried to strengthen the seat by placing heavy mending straps on the underside of the seat.

Glue was forced into the cracks and then the seat was clamped with pipe clamps while the glue dried. (Notice the holes left by the mending plate screws.)

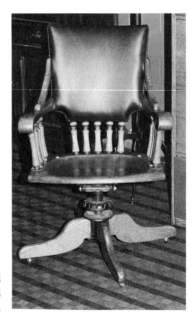

After the chair was repaired and refinished it was treated to professional reupholstering.

This detail shows the damage that can occur on an antique when framed panels shrink.

split panel together, then reassemble it with the framework, allowing the panel to slide freely in the channel.

You're faced with a bigger problem if the damaged panel is part of the permanent structure of a case piece. A typical example of this situation would be the lovely marble-topped early Victorian mahogany desk which stands in my study today. This desk spent the first one-hundred-plus years of its life in misty England, where the damp air prevented the wood from excessive drying. A returning serviceman shipped it to the United States after the end of World War II, and eventually it found its way to Colorado. When I bought it a couple of years ago, the exceptionally dry air here at our high altitude had taken its toll. A side panel had split, leaving a gaping 1/8-inch-wide crack. There was no way to get the panel out of the desk, and the glue would not release its hold.

The only solution was to cut a long wafer-thin sliver of mahogany and, after spreading glue along all edges, force it into that crack. I can still see the repair, even after touch-up refinishing but most people aren't aware of it.

When the split in a case piece is too thin to insert a wood strip, the only thing to do is fill the crack with wood dough or filler of a matching color.

Fortunately, the natural graining and variations in color of wood help disguise these repairs very nicely.

Hardware—Using It, Reusing It, Replacing It

Count yourself fortunate when you come upon an antique with all its original hardware. Few desks, chests, dressers, and cabinets survive the years with all their pulls, escutcheons, locks, and keys intact.

Excellent reproduction hardware is available at fairly reasonable prices, however. (Check the catalogs of the suppliers listed at the end of the book.) You can buy just about any piece of hardware you need cast in quite authentic period styles. Your only real problem may be in trying to decide just *which* of the pulls, knobs, handles, or whatever you want to use.

Make certain, though, that the new hardware you buy for an antique matches the style and period of that piece. A sure mark of a neophyte restorer is delicate Queen Anne pulls on a late Victorian chest or Hepplewhite escutcheons on a Mission Oak bookcase. Study style books in a library and the antiques in museums to absorb this knowledge.

Antiquing New Hardware Most of the reproduction hardware you buy will be too new to look authentic on an antique. And only an amateur or someone who really doesn't care about antiques would put some of this flashy hardware on a lovely old piece of furniture. Several ways exist, though, to "age" new brass hardware. I'll share two of the simplest ones with you. First, use a pair of pliers to carefully hold the piece of hardware over a burning candle until the brass is smoked and black. Take a rag and gently wipe some of the black off, leaving enough to give an old and slightly tarnished look to the brass. Spray on a couple of coats of waterproof lacquer to seal the black onto the brass.

The second method calls for a commercial fluid especially made to mottle brass. You wipe the fluid on with a rag or cottonball,

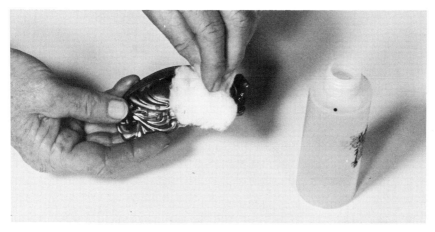

You can "antique" new reproduction hardware with a commercial product especially made for this purpose. It will eliminate the objectionable brassy finish in minutes.

allow it to cure a few minutes, then rinse off. No protective spray is necessary.

DUPLICATING OLD HARDWARE   Quite often I will find a lovely antique which has all but one or two of the original pulls or knobs. This was the case with the pretty little Eastlake commode on the cover of this book. It was missing one pull out of four originals when I found it. It would have been a crime to discard three original pieces of hardware in favor of replacing the set with four matching reproductions. The solution was to have the missing one copied.

Only the workers at a brass foundry can do this copying successfully. Look in your Yellow Pages for a foundry in your area. You'll have to take one of the old pieces of hardware to them to use for a mold, but the duplicate will be exactly like the original, even down to the natural oxidation of the metal. The cost of having hardware copied does not fit into the bargain basement category. In fact, the bill for that one pull was as much as I would have spent to buy four new matching reproductions. But I felt it was money well spent to retain the authenticity of the commode. Any antique with its original hardware is more valuable than one with reproduction hardware.

REACTIVATING OLD LOCKS   Almost all antique desks, chests, dressers, and cabinets were built with locks on the doors and drawers. Often these locks seem to be jammed, but you can nearly always free them up. Get a can of any silicone lubricant and spray the liquid generously into the lock. Take the original key, if you have it, or a reproduction and gently "work" the lock until it opens smoothly. I've never failed to get a lock working by using this method. Most old keys have long since disappeared, however, by the time we come upon an antique in need of restoration. You can buy new ones from one of the suppliers listed at the end of the book. They offer several styles and each is listed in the catalog with the type of furniture it will fit—kitchen cabinet, desk, dresser, etc. Most of these old locks are quite generic, so you shouldn't have any trouble getting a key to fit any lock.

REPLACING CASTERS All antique office chairs, as well as many tables and case pieces, were built to accommodate casters. Time and hard wear, though, have dealt a hard blow to many of these quite practical rollers. Replacing them is a cinch, however, unless the wood which surrounded the original metal socket is badly deteriorated.

Let's take the easy cases first. Very often you'll find a chair or table with the casters missing but the metal socket still intact and in good condition. All you have to do then is just insert new casters into the old sockets. I've done this many times and had no trouble at all with the mechanism working perfectly.

You may, though, find both sockets and casters missing. In that case you'll find a hole drilled into the base of the leg. Measure that hole for depth and diameter to make sure it will accommodate a new socket. Most new sockets require a hole 1½ inches deep and ⅜ inch in diameter. If the socket you're working with is smaller than that, drill it out to that measurement. If it is considerably larger, plug it with a dowel and redrill, as described in another section of this chapter. Then insert the new socket and caster. If the original hole is just a trifle over ⅜ inch in diameter, you can fill out the extra space with wood dough. Assemble the caster's stem into the socket *before* you insert it into the leg. Push a wad of wood dough into the new hole and press the assembled caster and socket firmly into the dough, making sure the teeth engage either the wood or the wood dough. Flip the roller around several times to make sure it will move freely once the dough hardens.

Now, how do you handle the situation if the sockets are missing and the wood at the base of the legs is partially rotted away? This is quite common with furniture which stood in damp basements too long. You can't drill satisfactorily into wood which is loose and crumbling. You can, though, rebuild that wood until it is solid enough to support the socket and caster.

One way is to scrape away the soft wood and fill the resulting cavity with wood dough. Then cut a piece of thin wood to the same dimensions as the leg. Nail or screw this piece of wood onto the bottom of the leg to act as a cap. Once the wood dough is dry and firm, sand the cap and any visible wood dough to conform to the original design of the leg. Now, drill a ⅜-inch hole through this cap and the hardened dough. Insert the new metal socket into the hole, then add the caster.

You can even level a piece of furniture that tilts a bit by making the cap for the short leg a bit thicker than for the others. I did this for the bookcase on the cover of this book. Not only were the legs badly worn, but one was a full ½ inch shorter than the others by the time I got the bookcase repaired and squared up. (I haven't the foggiest idea where that ½ inch went!)

Now you may someday come upon a fine old office chair or cabinet with one or more legs deteriorated to the point that the above repair method isn't feasible. In that case, the only practical solution is to trim the legs down to the solid wood. You can then add enough new wood to bring the leg or legs to the former dimensions. Or, simply attach the casters to the newly cut bottom of the legs. You can do this if the comfort or design of the piece of furniture does not depend upon that wood you cut away. In most cases an inch or two missing from the height of a cabinet makes no difference at all in its usefulness or design. That isn't the case with some chairs, but you will never miss that bit of length from the legs if you are working with an office chair which has a mechanism to adjust the height. You can compensate for the wood you cut away by raising the seat an inch or so. I've done this several times, and in no way damaged the beauty or practicality of the chair.

TIGHTENING HINGES The doors to commodes and other case pieces usually are attached to the body of the piece of furniture

Replacement hardware for antique beds comes in two parts. One part is attached to the bed's legs, and the other part to the end of the new rails. The section which is attached to the bed legs must be placed over slots cut into the wood. Drill and then chisel these slots about ½ inch deep. (Note in this photograph the slot left from the original hardware.)

Screw the new plate over the slots.

Attach the corresponding plate to the ends of the new rail. This plate hooks into the one screwed to the bed's legs. The resulting joint is quite secure.

with tiny hinges and even tinier screws. These little screws nearly *always* work loose in time, resulting in a dragging door. All you have to do to shore up the door is to remove the screws, insert a piece of wooden matchstick into the screw hole, add a squirt of glue, and then reinsert the screws. Easiest repair you'll ever make!

LENGTHENING BED RAILS Most beds made a century or more ago were several inches shorter than our modern beds. Therefore, the old rails, even if in good condition, will not allow the use of a ready-made commercial box spring and mattress. You can, of course, have a mattress company construct a custom-made mattress and box spring to fit the bed.

It's far more practical, and easier than you think, to make new rails. Buy two solid planks, 1 in. x 6 in. x 6 ft. 4 in., in the same hardwood as the bed. Attach new hardware to the end of the new rails and to the head- and footboards as illustrated here. This hardware is available from one of the suppliers listed at the end of the book.

You can buy metal mattress supports which hook over the top of the rail to hold the box spring in place. Or you can attach wooden supports of 2 in. x 2 in. x 4 ft. stock to the insides of the rails. The latter method adds an hour or so to the repair time, but it does result in a more authentic-looking antique.

OVERLARGE SCREW HOLES One common problem in repairing antique furniture is trying to reuse old screws (which I recommend) in holes which have become too large. The time-honored solution to this problem is to stick the end of a couple of wooden matchsticks into the hole, squirt in a bit of glue, and then reinsert the screw. This trick is just about foolproof.

EMBEDDED SCREWS On the other hand, if a screw seems to have taken up permanent residence in a piece of antique furniture, here are some suggestions to get the thing to *release* its grip.

First, try to lubricate the screw and its hole with a few drops of kerosene or the commercial liquid especially made to loosen stubborn screws. Allow the lubricant to soak into the wood for an hour or so, reapplying several times.

Then use a sturdy screwdriver whose blade tip fits the screw's slot exactly. A screwdriver that is too small may damage the slot, sometimes terminally. Put all your weight behind the screwdriver, pressing down on the screw as you try to turn the screwdriver counterclockwise.

No luck? Don't despair. Put the screwdriver tip back in the screw's slot and strike the end of the handle with a hammer as hard as you can without dislodging the screwdriver and mashing your hand. Then take a nail set in your left hand and place its tip at the far right-hand side of the slot, holding the tool almost parallel to the flat head of the screw. Again, use your hammer, this time striking the blunt end of the nail set, trying to force the screw counterclockwise. If anything will break the hold of a stubborn screw, it is the combination of lubricant, a sharp blow, and the leverage action of the nail set.

Sometimes you'll come upon an old screw whose slot has been obliterated by years of rust, grime, or paint. You can cut a new slot by literally sawing through the gunk with a hacksaw blade. Be careful, though. Old metal can be pretty soft, and it is easy to cut too deeply into the screw. Then you'll *really* have trouble!

REUSING OLD SCREWS It's always a good idea to reuse old screws whenever possible in repairing antique furniture. The shine on new screws screams "repair!" and really detracts from the over-all appearance of the piece. So save all the screws you remove from old furniture, and watch for coffee cans full of old screws at garage sales. I pounce on these as though they were made of gold!

These old screws will go into wood just as easily as new ones if you lubricate them first. All you have to do is twirl the screw a time or two across a cake of soft soap or dip it in lubricating oil or dishwashing detergent. In fact, I usually lubricate all screws, even new ones. It's amazing how easily they will glide into even the hardest wood after this treatment.

DISGUISING SCREW HOLES Most of the furniture makers who made the antiques of today were perfectionists. They took a great deal of pride in turning out *finished*-looking work. You'll seldom find, for instance, the raw heads of screws exposed anywhere except perhaps on hip rests and the backs of chair side posts. As you try to emulate the old-time quality make an effort to conceal all screws, too.

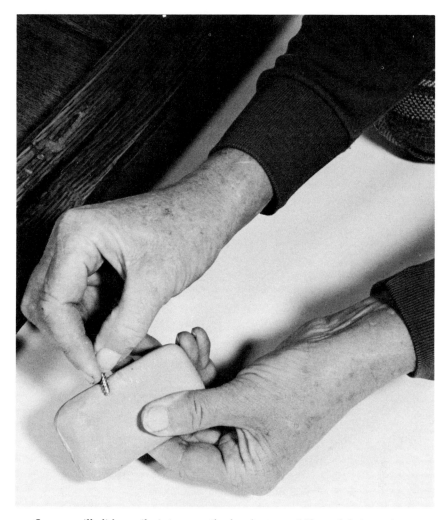

Screws will slide easily into even the hardest wood if you lubricate them first by drawing the screw across a cake of soap.

All screws on exposed surfaces should be countersunk, and then the holes should be plugged. Ready-made plugs come in a variety of woods and two styles, button and flat. Use the button style when you would like to add a little decorative detail to the antique. Use the flat type when you want to hide the fact that you put a screw into the wood at that spot. Either button or flat plugs can be

Countersink the hole for any screw which is inserted on an exposed surface.

Once the screw is in place, squirt a little wood glue in the depression and insert a wooden plug. Plugs come in several different woods and sizes.

finished to match the body of the piece, but remember, they are of new wood and lack the patina of old wood. You'll probably have to blend two different batches of oil, as described in Chapter 6, to get a good match.

REPLACING MISSING PARTS

Earlier in this book I said an antique's value could be diminished if any original section was replaced with a new part. This statement is certainly true. The admonition applies most especially, though, to those rare pieces which, for some reason, are exceptional examples of their periods. These are the antiques destined for soft berths today as museum-quality exhibits.

Garden-variety antiques, however, those with which this book is concerned, have about as much chance of making it to the Metropolitan Museum of Art as Lizzie Borden had of being selected Miss Congeniality of 1892. They've been hauled from Pennsylvania to Oregon in jolting wooden-wheeled wagons. They've made the journey to the gold camps of Colorado in the freight cars of narrow-gauge trains. They've been romped on by lively children and sat on by visiting aunts who were a bit too fond of the cream pot. They've been used as stepladders to reach top shelves where the jelly jars are stored, and dragged into barns to hold old horseshoes and spare tack.

Most of these antiques need some TLC, and that may well include replacing a broken or missing part. Now, no one who truly loves antiques will perform a "marriage" on them. This travesty is literally *building* an antique from scratch with several major parts taken from as many unrelated old pieces. The unforgivable sin! However, reality decrees that sometimes we must add a bit of wood or a small replacement part. By so doing, we can take a neglected and essentially worthless piece of old furniture and restore it to beauty and usefulness again.

REPLACING STRETCHERS AND SPINDLES Chairs receive the heaviest use of any piece of furniture in our homes, and so it is logical that antique chairs frequently arrive on our doorsteps with missing

This poor chair was picked up at a garage sale. Among its problems was a missing front stretcher.

Using the existing stretcher as a model, a custom woodworker turned a replacement stretcher on his lathe.

His skill enabled him to duplicate the stretcher exactly.

The seat of the chair had to be removed in order to insert the original and the replacement stretchers in the sockets.

The chair was then glued and reassembled before refinishing.

Once an ugly duckling, this sturdy and practical chair is now a lovely addition to the dining room.

parts. And, next to seats, those delicate members known as stretchers and spindles seem to be most in need of help.

The back and side stretchers that brace the legs of antique chairs often are just simple straight dowels. Replacing them is a cinch. All you have to do is measure the diameter of the ones still on the chair and buy dowel stock of the same size at your lumber company. Once home with the dowel, your first task will be to remove the old, dried glue out of the holes which held the old stretchers. The easiest way to do this is to drill the glue out with a drill bit the same size as the hole. You may find the splintered remains of an old stretcher still in the socket. Drill that out, too.

Now, cut the dowel to length, allowing for the distance it must extend into the chair legs. If it is too large to fit into the socket, trim the ends of this dowel with a utility knife, rasp (a rough file), or sandpaper. Rub glue around the ends of the dowel, squirt a little more into the socket, and set the new stretcher in place.

Sometimes you can spring a chair's legs apart enough to insert this new stretcher. More often, though, you'll have to take your rubber mallet and knock the legs apart. This will mean you'll loosen the other stretchers. You'll have to remove them all, sand their ends, drill out the old glue from the sockets, and reset them with glue too.

Most old chairs have elaborately turned *front* stretchers. If one or more of them is missing you'll have to duplicate it to restore the chair. The only practical way to duplicate a turned stretcher is on a modern lathe. Most of us do not have workshops equipped with the sophisticated and expensive machinery necessary to do this work. That's no real problem, though, since any custom woodworking shop can make duplicate replacement parts for a nominal fee. You take the stretcher you wish copied into the shop and the craftsperson there can turn out a duplicate in a matter of minutes. Just be sure to specify that he or she use the same type of wood from which the original part was made to construct the new one. A replacement turned stretcher is inserted into the sockets in the same way as a plain dowel, of course.

Inserting a replacement spindle into the back of a chair is usually more of a problem than that encountered with the stretchers. You'll have to knock the upright outer posts of the chair outward to release the top rail and so free the spindles. Unfortunately, many old chairs have had those top rails "tightened up" somewhere along the line—with nails. This so-called repair will quite effectively stop the removal of the rail. You'll have to dig those nails out as described earlier in this chapter.

Once any nails are out and the old glue is broken, that top rail should be easy to remove. Tap it off the top of the existing spindles. From this point on replacing a spindle is similar to replacing a stretcher.

REPLACING HIP RESTS Most old side chairs came equipped with hip rests, those curved pieces of wood which join the back and the seat at each side. Hip rests do *not* serve as a place to rest one's hips but as a brace between the back and seat of the chair. Without them the chair will be unsteady, and the back side posts will be in dire danger of breaking about 2 inches above the level of the seat. (I've found more than one antique chair with substantial cracks in the side posts from just this problem. Evidently some owner thought he or she could get away with using the chair after the hip rests had been burglarized for some other purpose.)

One or more of these hip rests *are* often missing from antique side chairs, but replacements are plentiful and not too expensive. You can order them from one of the suppliers listed at the end of the book.

You just attach the new hip rests to the chair's back and seat with screws. You'll even find the old screw holes still there to guide you in the proper placement. Now, these screws will be quite visible, so don't use shiny new steel ones. Use old screws or "age" new brass ones with one of the methods mentioned on page 80.

INTEGRATING NEW WOOD SECTIONS WITH OLD Every once in a while you'll find an antique which is missing some minor panel or piece of trim. The marble-topped walnut Eastlake commode on the cover of this book is one example. You'll notice in the "before" picture that a panel at the very bottom of the piece is missing. This panel was missing when I found the commode at a garage sale. Who knows how or why this integral part of a piece of furniture was removed. It had to be replaced, and the "after" picture shows the replacement panel in position.

The important thing to remember in constructing a new part for

The upright side posts of this chair were knocked outward and the top rail removed so an existing spindle could be removed to use as a pattern for the replacements.

The ends of any replacement stretcher or spindle will have to be trimmed to fit the existing socket.

an antique is to keep the design compatible with the body of the piece. For instance, when I was working on this commode a friend asked me why I didn't cut some attractive curves into the new panel. He couldn't understand why I was planning to glue on a perfectly straight board when I had a sabre saw in my basement workshop which could be used to fancy it up a bit. My answer was that nowhere on the lovely little antique had the original craftsman cut any curves, an austere philosophy typical of those who worked in Eastlake designs during the 1870s. So, I'll be willing to bet my bottle of yellow glue that the original panel had been a plain, straight board.

Keep this in mind when you're making a replacement part. You could easily ruin an antique's appearance by trying to "pretty it up."

The only problem I had in replacing that missing board was in trying to get the new wood to blend with the wood that was well over a hundred years old. My lumber dealer carries only one type of walnut in stock (which I bought) and evidently the commode was constructed of a different type because the colors were not even similar. The old wood had a richer, deeper brown tone than the new board, which had definite gray undertones. Add to that the issue of age and patina. Top it off with the fact that I had had to strip the commode to remove all the old paint and varnish. That altered the old wood's color to a certain extent.

At first glance it appeared I was working with two entirely different types of wood. But I put the replacement board in the hot summer sun and poured bleach and water on it for several days. Then I carefully mixed two blends of the colored finishing oils, putting one mixture on the new board and another on the old wood. The result was worth all the trouble because no one who has seen the commode has ever realized that piece of simple trim is not original.

I took care to use a straight board on that commode in order to preserve the design. I went to even more trouble to cut a curved replacement part for the vanity pictured here. This pretty 1920s vanity, while not a genuine antique according to the strictest stipulations, is still a useful and attractive piece of furniture. When I found it (painted bright pink, by the way!) the curved section on the lower part of the bottom right-hand drawer was broken off and missing. Fortunately, I had the other drawer to use as a pattern. A few minutes with my sabre saw and sander reproduced the fancy design. In making this replacement part I preserved not only the symmetry of the piece, but its quite feminine characteristics.

RECYCLING OLD PARTS AND WOOD   In the foregoing sections I discussed buying new wood replacement parts and using new

It is worth all the trouble involved to make a replacement part match the style of an antique, as illustrated by the unfinished lower drawer on the right side of this vanity.

wood stock to construct replacement parts for an antique. The only real problem you'll encounter in so doing is in trying to blend the colors of the old and new woods. Chapter 6 gives some hints on ways to do that.

You can sometimes bypass that little problem, though. One way is to reuse old parts. This is an especially practical alternative when restoring a chair. You'll often come upon broken-down chairs as you search for antiques to refinish. Useless as they are in their present condition, you can nearly always salvage a stretcher or two or a pair of hip rests from these chairs. I always seem to have at least one poor seatless, backless, or armless ruin hanging in my garage for just this purpose. There's no way these wrecks can be restored, but, considering the fifty cents or so I pay at garage sales, they're real bargains. The parts from these disasters are of oak or other hardwood, and have acquired that treasured patina of age. So, with just a little care, you can usually finish them to blend very nicely with your antique chair. Besides, you save yourself the trouble and expense of buying new parts.

Then, save all *scraps* of old wood. Keep a box in your workshop, garage, or utility room and throw in it every scrap of mellow wood you come by. And watch for such treasures as old table leaves, odd drawers, and other orphan pieces of furniture at garage sales. They're all invaluable when you need old wood to patch an antique or construct a replacement part.

REPLACING WOODEN ESCUTCHEONS

Many old pieces, especially those made of oak or walnut, were made with wooden instead of brass escutcheons. Placed as they were around keyholes, these thin pieces of wood took a lot of abuse. So you'll often find them missing or broken, as illustrated here. To replace them, you merely pry off any wood remaining from the original escutcheon, sand the area beneath well, and glue on the replacement. You can order replacements in several woods from the suppliers listed at the end of the book.

If it is properly finished to match the body of the antique, you

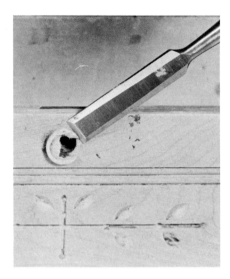

One of the escutcheons was missing from the Eastlake-style commode pictured on the cover of the book, and the other was damaged beyond repair. I removed the damaged one so replacements could be glued on.

The commercially available replacements are identical in style to the original escutcheons.

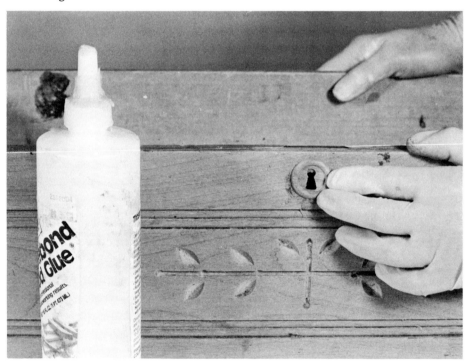

won't be able to tell the difference between this new escutcheon and any originals on the piece.

SHAPING CURVED CHAIR SLATS Many old office chairs were constructed with shaped back and side slats. Reproducing and installing a duplicate to take the place of a broken or damaged one certainly isn't the easiest of repairs. It can be done, though, and a few hours' effort will salvage a valuable chair for another century of use.

Your first step is to pry or drill out the remains of the damaged slat. Then make a pattern for the new slat, using one of the intact slats as a template. Press a piece of paper against the narrow dimension of the slat and reproduce its curve by drawing along it with a pencil. Transfer this pencil line, which duplicates the curving side of the slat, to a block of scrap wood at least as long as the slat. Cut along this pencil line with a sabre saw. The result will be two pieces of wood that fit together like the pieces of a jigsaw puzzle, whose inside edges exactly duplicate the curve of the slat. You will place a straight replacement slat in this curved jig you've made and shape it under pressure. You'll have better results if you laminate two thin slats rather than try to bend one of the finished thickness. Cut, or have your lumber company cut, two thin slats, each half the thickness, the same width, and 3 or 4 inches longer than the original slat. For instance, the exposed measurements of the slats in the chair illustrated were ½ in. x ¾ in. x 12 in. So I cut two thin slats, each ¼ in. x ¾ in. x 16 in. The extra 4 inches gave me plenty of wood to fit into the sockets plus some for trimming and an allowance for error.

To laminate and shape these slats, spread glue on one side of each slat, then press them together. Place a strip of waxed paper on either side of this wooden "sandwich" and put the whole thing between the curved edges of the jig. Clamp the jig together, forcing the slats to conform to its shape. Allow the laminated slat to harden overnight. Next day sand the edges and trim the ends to the desired length.

How you insert this replacement slat into the original sockets is largely determined by your chair. You may want to take the top rail off as described earlier in this chapter. Or you may try this: Cut a

One curved back slat was broken out of this interesting mahogany office chair.

The first step in replacing it was to drill and chisel out the broken remains of the old slat.

The curve of the existing slats was reproduced on paper and then transferred to scrap wood.

The next step was to cut along this penciled line. This gave me two pieces of wood which fit together with a curve exactly duplicating the curve of the existing slats.

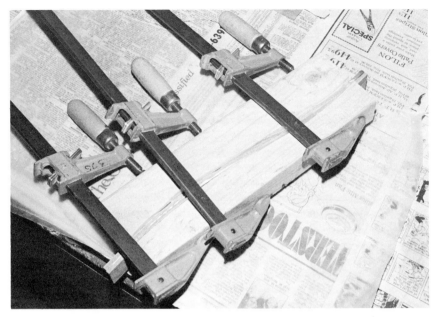

The two thin slats are glued together and forced into the curved jig under pressure. The replacement slat assumed and retained the curved shape once the glue was dry.

Once this chair is refinished it will be extremely difficult to tell the replacement slat from the originals.

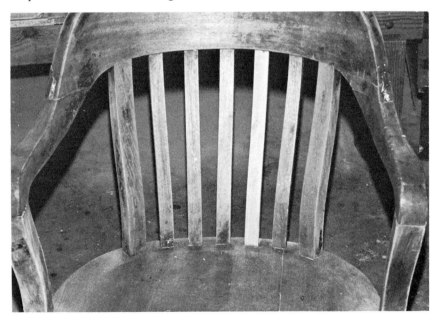

shallow channel in the wood of the seat behind the bottom socket. This gives you enough space to slide the new slat into the sockets with the top rail still in place. You will have to add some more new wood to fill in that channel, but it eliminates taking a very solid chair apart.

WORN AND STICKING DRAWERS

Someday you will undoubtedly acquire a chest or dresser whose drawers will become the bane of your existence. You'll be able to close them fairly well until about the last inch, when you have to lift them to complete the movement. While irritating, that little problem is at least an indication the antique is genuine! The trouble stems from the fact that drawer sides and the runners inside the dresser itself were usually made of softwood while the body of the dresser and the front of the drawer were made of hardwood. Through the years that softwood wore down, sometimes ¼ inch or more, while the hardwood front panels remained essentially unchanged. When you close the drawer, it slides along until it jams against the front panel. The only way to completely close the drawer is to lift it, allowing the front panel to clear the framework and slide in.

If the sides of the drawers are noticeably worn you can build them up to their original dimensions. Use a utility knife to shave thin slivers of wood to fit the worn area. Wooden paint stirrers, tongue depressors, and ice cream sticks also make good replacement parts. Once the shims, the new pieces of thin wood, are glued onto the bottom of the drawer, sand all surfaces smooth and finish off with a coat or two of varnish. Then rub the new edges with a cake of soap or spray with some lubricant to insure smooth gliding in the future.

Runners wear down almost as often as drawers. These little strips of wood stretch from front to back inside the body of the antique, supporting the drawers. If the runners are stationary, simply add slivers of wood to them with glue as described above. If they are removable, just try turning them over. You may find an adequately smooth surface there. If not, I'd suggest making new runners by cutting new wood to the measurements of the runners. That would be far simpler than trying to build up the old ones.

After you get the drawers closing efficiently you may find they go too *far* into the piece of furniture. If so, chances are the stops have fallen out. These stops are just small pieces of wood, usually a 1-inch-long piece of 1 in. x 1 in. wood, glued inside the back of the drawer cavity. To replace them you need to locate the marks left by the original stops. As a rule you can find these areas without trouble because there will be a difference in the patination of the wood at those spots. Or there may be bits of old dried glue still clinging to the wood there. If you can't find the old stop marks, just measure the depth of the drawer front to back. Then measure the drawer cavity front to back the same distance and place a pencil mark at that point. Glue your stops behind the pencil mark. This will keep the drawer from sliding in too far.

CORRECTING WARPAGE IN FURNITURE

Furniture warps when one surface of the piece (the convex side) absorbs more moisture than does the opposite surface (the concave side). You can usually correct this common problem in antique furniture if the warped piece is removable.

This is one repair job where stripping is absolutely necessary. Remove every bit of paint, varnish, oil, wax, or other finish so wood fibers will be free to absorb moisture, then dry uniformly.

Your goal is to add moisture to the dry side, and gradually allow the piece to dry under pressure. This helps the wood stabilize both its moisture content and form. You don't need professional equipment to correct a warp, either a below-ground concrete floor or a shady spot on the lawn will do nicely.

If working on the concrete floor of your basement, you soak several towels in water, wring them out, and lay the warped board, separated from its base, on the wet towels. Place the board concave side down. That is, if the board is warped so its edges bow upward you put it on the towels with the edges *down*. Place heavy weights, concrete blocks or bricks work nicely, on the upper side of the warped board. Shut the door and let nature take over.

Depending upon the amount of warp, you should see results in a couple of days. Once the board appears to be flat and level, lift it, remove the towels, turn the board over, and lay it down on the same spot. Some moisture should remain in the concrete, enough to continue the re-forming process. If not, dampen the concrete and replace the weights. Continue this daily turning of the top for three or four more days. At that point the board should be about as flat as it will ever be and ready for the final drying. Take it to a warm, dry room and continue turning and weighting it down for a few more days.

Reassemble the top and its base, then, using good quality wood glue and hidden screws. Refinish the piece. Seal the underside of the board as well as its top side to help forestall any more problems in the future.

You don't have a damp basement at your place? How about a flat spot on the lawn? Soak a section of your lawn with the garden hose. Lay a cotton sheet on the ground to protect the wood from dirt and grass stains and follow the procedure described above, weighting and turning the top for about a week. Then move it to a dry, but still shady, spot in the yard for the last few days of drying, again turning and weighting as described above.

REPAIRING MAJOR BREAKS IN WOOD

One of your primary objectives when restoring antique furniture is to make a repair without any external evidence of that repair. Professional restorers often use a repair technique called blind dowels to achieve this result. The repair is strong, invisible, and actually quite simple to master. You'll find it especially valuable when faced with a broken chair or table leg, or with a split chair seat.

This repair involves joining the broken pieces with one or more hardwood dowels. First remove any broken sections still attached to the body of the furniture. Gather the sections and place them on

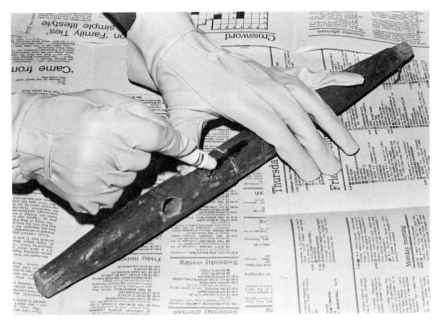

Align the broken edges and draw a mark across the break. This mark will help you realign the parts.

Drill a hole into one side of the break. Center it at that line you drew.

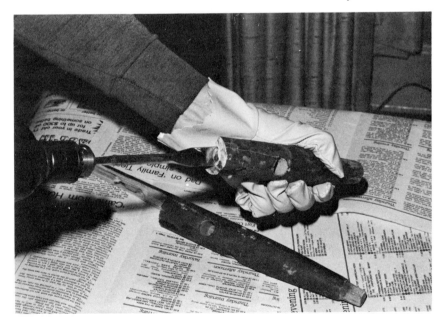

a flat surface, aligning them at the break. Take a pencil and draw one line *across* the break of a narrow chair leg, drawing several distinct lines for a thicker table leg. Separate the broken pieces. Using a drill bit the diameter of the dowel you'll use for the repair, drill holes ½ inch to 1 inch deep (depending on the thickness of the leg) into only one side of the break.

No formula exists for the correct size dowel to use in any specific situation, but a good rule of thumb would be to use one about one-third the diameter of the broken piece.

Cut a dowel, one for each line you drew, into lengths twice as long as the depth of the drill hole. For instance, if you drilled a ½-inch hole, you would cut each dowel into 1-inch lengths. Brush glue onto half of the dowel and tap it into the hole you drilled; the remaining half of the dowel should protrude from the break.

Using the line you drew across the break as a guide, align the broken sections again. At the point where the protruding dowel touches the remaining section, trace the circumference of the dowel. Drill out this spot to the same depth you drilled the first hole.

Brush glue on the projecting end of the dowel and along both sides of the break. Tap the two sections together, using the lines as a guide, and you should have a perfect match and a virtually in-visible repair. Wipe the excess glue off, clamp, and allow the repair to dry overnight.

TIGHTENING OLD WICKER

Wicker furniture sometimes becomes a bit loose, and the seats start to sag after many pleasant summers on the front porch. You can often firm it up without doing any major repair work. Just take the piece to the backyard and scrub it down with a mixture of hot water, vinegar, and laundry soap. Rinse well with the garden hose and allow the piece to dry outdoors. The canes will shrink and tighten as they dry, usually leaving you with a much more sub-stantial piece of furniture. The same technique works to firm up saggy cane seats on chairs. Glue any broken pieces of cane into place, then spray with a good quality exterior paint.

Glue and tap a dowel into the hole, then press the other side of the break against the protruding end of the dowel. Draw a line around the spot where the dowel touches the broken wood.

Drill a hole at the area indicated by the spot. Put glue in the hole and press the two parts of the break together. Use that line you drew across the break to help you line the parts up perfectly.

REPAIRING DAMAGED VENEER

Veneering is the process of glueing a thin layer of expensive cabinet wood to a base of ordinary wood. As furniture ages, the glue between these layers loosens either from excess moisture or dryness. The edges of an old veneered piece are often chipped or warped. Many times small pieces of the veneer will be missing. While only an experienced professional can restore badly damaged veneer to its original state, you can repair some minor damage yourself.

BLISTERS Veneer blisters look like bubbles, small areas where the glue has loosened surrounded by large areas of firmly affixed veneer. These bubbles are easy to see. The veneer will be raised slightly above the base wood at that spot, and often the blisters can be pressed down with slight pressure from a finger.

Faced with such a blister on veneer, your first try at repairing it should be to simply *iron* it down. Wet the blister first with hot water, then place waxed paper or a brown paper bag over the spot. Top with two or three thicknesses of a folded rag. Turn your dry household iron to a medium setting and place it on the folded cloth. Leave it there for thirty seconds or so. Remove the cloth and paper and immediately place a large cold item, a cast-iron skillet, for instance, on the blister. Weight it down and allow it to set overnight. What you've done is soften the old glue with heat and then harden it again with the sudden cooling and pressure.

If that doesn't work, you can try this: Take a razor blade and carefully slit through the center of the blister along the grain of the wood. Lay a hot, wet cloth on the blister for a few minutes. Once the wood feels damp and flexible, carefully slip a table knife under one side of the slit. Lift the knife to raise one side of the slit. Press some glue under the raised side. Remove the table knife and repeat the process on the other side of the slit. Wipe off any excess glue, cover with waxed paper, and firmly weight down the repair over-night or until the wood is thoroughly dry.

MISSING VENEER   Pieces of veneer sometimes break off the edges of tables, often at corners. You can patch this damage but the results may not be completely to your liking.

Clamp a piece of replacement veneer, available from suppliers listed at the end of the book, over the damaged area, allowing ½ inch or so of extra material all around. With a razor blade, X-Acto knife, or utility knife cut through both the new veneer and the old. Cut with the grain along one side of the repair and in a straight line when going across the grain.

Release the clamp, remove the new patch, any scrap veneer from the patch, and the old, damaged veneer. Sand away any dried glue that remains in the area to be patched. Your patch of new veneer should fit perfectly into the section cut out of the old veneer.

Now measure the thickness of the old veneer against the re-placement patch. You may find that the new veneer is much thin-ner than the old. In this case, you'll have to cut another two or

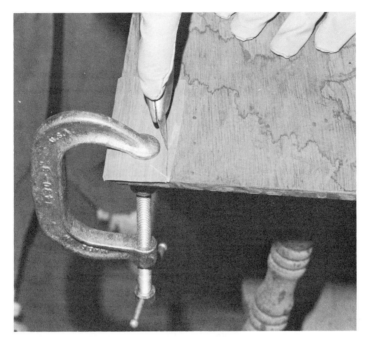

A small piece of veneer had broken off the edge of this table. A piece of replacement veneer was put over the damaged area and a patch was cut, working through both the replacement veneer and the original veneer. By cutting through both the new and the old veneer at the same time, I was able to make the patch exactly duplicate the area into which it would fit.

three sections of veneer to bring the patch up to the level of the old veneer.

Spread a layer of contact cement onto the core wood, wait the recommended time, and place one of the patches onto it. Repeat with more contact cement and another patch. Repeat until you've built up to the thickness of the original veneer. Make sure the grain of the final piece of veneer patch follows the grain of the body of the furniture top.

Clean off any excess cement, allow the cement to set for an hour or two, then trim the edges.

CHIPPED VENEER Sometimes tiny chips of veneer will be broken off raggedly along the edge of a tabletop or dresser. The only reasonably attractive solution to this problem that I know of is to sand the broken edge of veneer back, canting the sander down at about a 45-degree angle. Carefully done, this technique results in a smooth edge, even though the angle formed by the top and sides of the piece will be quite different from the original angle. You *could* trim the veneer back and insert a new strip along the edge, but this repair would be highly visible and unattractive.

LIFTED EDGES OF VENEER   Frequently veneer will lift from the core wood along the edges of an antique without any pieces breaking off. This problem is usually the easiest of all to repair. First clean the space between the veneer and core wood to remove any dirt lodged there. Insert contact cement into this cavity, wait the time recommended by the manufacturer before pressing down firmly. Cover the area with waxed paper, place a long board on top to equalize pressure, and then clamp. I recommend this last step just to make sure the cement adheres all along the edge of the piece.

REPLACING AN ENTIRE VENEER TOP   You can put a completely new veneer top on an antique if you're willing to take the time and trouble. Veneer is available in many different woods, several sizes and thicknesses, and a wide range of prices.

Actually putting the new veneer on is the easy part. Removing the old veneer is the hard part. Old veneer glue can be very tenacious. However, you may feel your antique justifies the effort if its top is too badly damaged to repair, yet the piece is worth saving.

Using any thin-bladed tool such as a utility knife, putty knife, or spatula, begin prying the veneer off the core wood around the edges. Expect to hit a great deal of resistance once you get past the first few inches. At that point you can try dissolving the old glue. One of the best solutions for this job is full-strength, boiling vinegar. Plan on using at least a gallon of white vinegar for the average 24 in. × 24 in. table. Wearing rubber gloves to protect your hands, turn the table over on its side and carefully pour the boiling vinegar along the edges of the veneer, trying to pry it up at the same time. This process may take quite a while. If the glue doesn't release its hold after the first application of vinegar, wait fifteen minutes and try again. You might have to make several applications.

Let the table dry completely once you get all the old veneer off. Then sand away every scrap of glue that remains on the core wood. Fill any gouges with wood putty and sand again. The surface must be smooth and clean for the new veneer to adhere.

Measure and cut a piece of veneer at least ½ inch longer and wider than the surface you are covering.

Apply a coat of quality contact cement to the surface of the table. One manufacturer of cement especially made for veneer work recommends using a small roller for this job. Let the cement dry approximately thirty minutes then test it by pressing a piece of paper onto the adhesive. If the paper does not stick you're ready to proceed. Apply a coat of contact cement to the back of the veneer. Allow it to sit for about fifteen minutes. Test it as above, but now you want it to be slightly tacky.

Cut a sheet of heavy paper at least ½ inch larger than the surface of the table. Place this "slip sheet" over the surface of the table to separate the veneer from the base until it is in position. Put the veneer on top of the slip sheet.

Carefully, a few inches at a time, slip the paper from under the veneer. Enlist someone's help before attempting this, because once that veneer with its coat of cement touches the cement-covered base it will stick—permanently! You will *not* be able to reposition it.

Smooth the veneer in the direction of the grain as you slowly slip the paper, inch by inch, from between it and the base. Take your time.

Once you're through, take a deep breath, sit down and relax for half an hour. Then go back and trim the edges with a razor or X-Acto knife. Wait at least twenty-four hours before sanding and finishing.

BROKEN MARBLE

You can *refinish* marble, as you'll learn in the next chapter, but only a professional can successfully *repair* broken or badly damaged marble. These talented people can work wonders, though.

Check your Yellow Pages for the name of a company that specializes in repairing marble. You'll find them listed under "Marble" or "Monuments." Take the damaged piece to them, and, chances are, they'll return it to you unblemished and beautifully polished.

They can join broken pieces with a mastic that closely resembles the marble's natural graining, making the repair virtually undetectable. They can even fill in small missing sections with a marble-like substance. They can rebuild chipped edges or trim the edges down, cutting a lovely new pattern in the process. Don't expect them to replace large missing pieces, though.

Only a skilled craftsperson can do this work, so these repairs are not cheap. Expect to pay anywhere from $30 for a minor job to well over $100 for a major renovation.

❦ 6 ❦

GENERAL REFINISHING TECHNIQUES

Perhaps your most useful knowledge in refinishing antique furniture will be an understanding of the various characteristics of the different cabinet woods. I suggest you stop in at some good lumber company and ask to see the sample display of raw and finished lumber. Seeing and touching actual samples can show you, far better than any words of mine, the diversity of these woods. You can compare the open grain of oak to the closed grain of rosewood. You'll see which woods are almost white in their natural states and which ones have a distinct brown or reddish tint. You'll notice how these colors react to finishing oils and stains.

Every lumber company has a scrap bin, so while you're there ask for a few small pieces of these cabinet woods to take home with you. You can then make your own comparison tests. Put a little penetrating oil on a piece of ash and then the same amount on mahogany. You'll notice they don't absorb the oil at the same rate, and one will absorb quite a bit more than the other. Hit a piece of oak with a hammer, and then hit a piece of poplar with the same force. You'll see quite graphically that one would resist the ravages of time while the other would soon become worn and scarred in daily household use. Cut geometrically identical pieces of pine and walnut. Notice the difference in their weights.

The following chart lists some of the basic characteristics of the most popular cabinet woods which have been used in antique furniture.

WOOD	COLOR	DENSITY	GRAIN	DISTINGUISHING CHARACTERISTICS
Ash	light, creamy	medium	wavy, close	veined, streaks in direction of growth
Beech	light brown	medium	straight	easily worked, takes color well
Birch	cream or reddish brown	heavy	plain or curly	similar to maple
Butternut	light brown	soft	close	similar to walnut
Cherry	reddish brown	medium to hard	straight or curly	similar to some mahogany
Chestnut	brownish yellow	medium	straight	similar to some oak
Hickory	cream	hard	fine, straight	tough, resilient
Holly	light	hard	close	mostly used for marquetry and inlay
Mahogany	light to dark reddish brown	hard	straight to wavy	attractive grain, durable, often in wide pieces, popular for veneer
Maple	rich, light brown	hard	close, straight, curly, birdseye	strong, heavy
Oak	light cream to light brown	hard	open, straight to wavy	heavy, tough
Pine	light, creamy	soft	straight	resinous, flexible, often used for core wood
Poplar	yellow to brownish yellow	medium	straight, close	even texture, barely visible pores, takes color well
Rosewood	blackish brown	hard	wavy, close	pleasant fragrance
Satinwood	yellowish	medium	straight	lustrous surface
Tulipwood	light	medium	straight to wavy	pink stripes
Walnut	grayish brown to rich brown	hard	straight	strong, easily worked

These differences in wood determine, among other things, the way woods react to certain finishes. An understanding of these differences will help you know in advance, for instance, that a walnut table will become darker when treated with a certain color of oil than would a pine table. This would happen because walnut is naturally darker in tone than pine. You would know that a chestnut cabinet would absorb more oil, and therefore probably be darker, than would an oak cabinet since the chestnut has less density than the oak.

Once you become really knowledgeable about these differences in wood you'll be able to control final colors to your satisfaction. For instance, you could take an oak dining table, a set of ash chairs, a chestnut commode, and a pine buffet (all made at different times by different craftsmen) and refinish them so the colors would be almost identical. If you tried to use the same blend of oil on all you'd end up with a dining room full of mismatched colors instead of a harmonious grouping that will be a pleasure to use and live with.

Too, you'll discover if you already haven't, that some furniture makers of the past had a very cavalier attitude about mixing various woods in the *same* piece of furniture. Many's the time I've discovered a couple of oak panels in an otherwise all-walnut cabinet or a mahogany occasional table whose bottom shelf turned out to be maple. Those old craftsmen know how to mix their stains to make diverse woods blend as one. You can do the same in refinishing the pieces today.

Probably the most frequent use I have for this skill is when trying to blend the color of a new replacement dowel with that of a century-old chair. My lumber company carries plain dowels in walnut, oak, and birch. Many of the pretty press-back chairs I find, though, are made of ash. So I have to be able to blend oils that will make oak look like ash.

Too, old wood takes color differently than does new wood, even if they are of the same variety. Any new piece of wood inserted into an antique, whether a spindle, patch, or whatever, will be several shades lighter than the old wood. So its sharp, clean tone must be blended in with the older, more mellow tone with two different shades of oil. You can learn to do this by experimenting with scraps of new and old wood of different varieties.

TO STRIP OR NOT TO STRIP?

That is indeed the question, and you'll hear contrasting opinions about the subject as you get more into this hobby. One theory says you should never remove the original finish of an antique. And undoubtedly, an antique in good condition with its original finish is certainly one to be desired and cherished. The other side of the discussion agrees but also argues that many, many antiques have finishes no one but a nurturing alligator could love. Actually, both theses are correct.

You should certainly try to save the finish of any antique you find whose original finish has not been painted over. I once assumed that *any* antique with a darkened and rough finish had to be stripped before it could be renovated. After much useless work, I discovered that a great many of these unattractive finishes could be restored to their original beauty *without* stripping.

Many antiques appear to be black because years of grime and furniture polish have created that thick opaque covering. Often it takes only a good cleaning to revitalize the finish. However, if someone has painted the antique or if the old finish is in really deplorable condition you have no choice but to strip off all the finish and start over.

Begin by cleaning the antique with a mild soap and water solution, applied with a soft fiber brush. Do not soak the piece as you could easily dissolve the old glue. *Never* put water on any antique that you suspect might have inlays or marquetry, or one with a veneered surface.

Allow the wood to dry. Working in a well-ventilated area, go over the wood thoroughly with a rag soaked well in paint thinner, turpentine, or carbon tetrachloride. You may notice a distinct lightening of the color. You can sometimes remove more dirty old finish by rubbing the wood with a mixture of linseed oil and powdered pumice. Put a few spoonsful of pumice in a container and add linseed oil until the mixture has the consistency of thick cream.

Thoroughly clean any antique before you decide to strip it. You may find that only dirt and furniture polish obscure its natural beauty.

Caution! *Never* use flammable cleaners in any enclosed space unless you can open the doors or windows. *Never* allow anyone to light a match, smoke, or cause a spark near these solvents. It is safest to work outdoors and then leave the piece of furniture out there until all flammable solvent has evaporated from the wood.

The finish on old furniture sometimes acquires an unpleasant pebbled roughness with time. You can often remove this graininess by dissolving the old finish with its original solvent. The process is called amalgamation.

Most antiques were finished with shellac, the standard with furniture makers until well into the 1920s. Shellac dissolves in denatured alcohol. To find if your antique was finished with shellac, you dip a pad of fine steel wool into some denatured alcohol and rub a concealed area. If the rough surface begins to smooth out under light pressure, the finish is, indeed, shellac.

You must work quickly when smoothing an old finish by amalgamation, since alcohol evaporates very quickly. Dip the pad of fine steel wool into the alcohol and rub it briskly over the finish, working in the direction of the grain. Add more alcohol as necessary to keep the surface wet, continually moving the steel wool pad with moderate pressure over the surface. The defects and pebbling of the old finish will begin to dissolve in front of your eyes. Turn the steel wool pad as necessary to keep it clean and unclogged. As soon as you are satisfied with the smoothness of the finish go back over it with clean alcohol and a fresh pad.

You can buy prepared commercial amalgamators which also do an excellent job of removing an old dark and wrinkled finish. They are quite expensive, though, considering the amount it takes to rejuvenate most antiques.

Amalgamation, whether with alcohol or a commercial product, results in a fine, lustrous finish which preserves the deep patina of the wood. Once cleaned, you need only polish the wood to restore its original beauty.

If you find that the finish did *not* dissolve readily with shellac you might try the same process with lacquer thinner. If that works, then the finish is lacquer. It is highly unlikely that you will find lacquer on a genuine antique, however. It was almost never used until the 1920s.

Almost every town has at least one firm which can strip paint from furniture. These companies can be a blessing when you're faced with a lovely old piece which is covered with multiple coats of pink, ivory, gold, and green enamel. Their powerful commercial solvents and equipment can cut through numerous layers and return a piece of furniture devoid of *any* paint, varnish, or finish.

However, you don't need a professional stripper for every antique in need of stripping. The solvents they use are powerful; they can sometimes dissolve the old glue right along with the paint. And on occasion, if the worker has to dip the piece too many times, the solvent can eat into the pores of the wood itself.

You do have the option of doing your own stripping, as I often do, using one of the commercial strippers available at any paint or hardware store. These thick liquids remove layers of old varnish in just a few minutes. They are not always as effective or fast on multiple layers of paint, though.

You'll find two kinds of strippers on the market today. One can be washed off with water; the other must be removed with paint thinner. Both are equally effective, but I prefer the water-soluble type for two reasons. First, water is less expensive for the rinsing process than paint thinner. Second, I try to avoid as many caustic and flammable substances as possible. Always follow the manufacturer's directions carefully when using a stripper.

First, you apply a thick coat of stripper to the wood, brushing in one direction only. You don't have to worry about going with the grain. Allow the stripper time to work. Sometimes you'll see results in five minutes, sometimes you may have to wait twenty minutes or more. The time you wait depends not only on the thickness and condition of the finish but also on air temperature and humidity.

When the varnish or paint wrinkles up and appears to lift from the surface of the wood you're ready to scrape the resulting goo off with a spatula or stiff brush. You can use a wire brush on hardwoods without damaging the piece as long as you work with the grain. Use an old toothbrush to get into the deep crevices of carvings and elaborate turnings. Once you have most of the old finish and remover off you're ready for the rinsing step. Depending upon the type of stripper you used, go back over the piece of furniture with a stiff fiber brush and either hot, sudsy water or paint thinner. Rinse off quickly and allow the antique to dry in the open air but out of the sun.

Once in a while you'll find that stripping does not remove all the paint from the pores of an open-grained wood. In that case you might try this little trick to lift the paint from the pores. Mix equal amounts of shellac and denatured alcohol and brush this mixture into the areas which still contain the paint. Allow the shellac to remain on the wood for a few days, then repeat the stripping process on those areas. This sometimes works. If it doesn't, the only solution I know of is to literally pick the tiny bits of paint from the pores with an X-Acto knife. This is a tedious job I've had to perform more times than I care to remember.

You may someday be faced with an antique which was finished with a milk paint. This popular and expensive nineteenth-century finish is almost impossible to remove. Made by boiling milk with either brick dust or animal blood, it was poured hot onto the bare wood. It made an attractive and durable deep red stain which is quite distinctive. In most cases, you would be better off to leave it as is. If you really want to change the color you might try stripping the piece of furniture and then lightening the red residue by bleaching, as described below.

Some of those eager homeowners also occasionally applied regular paint directly onto bare wood. Again, the paint usually soaked deeply and permanently into the pores of the wood. Even commercial stripping often won't remove all that color.

BLEACHING STAINS FROM WOOD

Someday you may need to lighten all or part of the wood in an antique. Tabletops acquire stains through the years. Sometimes natural dark streaks detract from the beauty of wood. Often stripping doesn't remove enough residue from an old stain (as mentioned in the preceding section) to allow the use of a lighter color in refinishing. And old desks and office chairs frequently arrive in our workshops complete with deep blue ink stains, reminders of the days before ball-point pens. Some form of bleaching will usually take care of these problems.

Professional furniture refinishers use a two-step bleaching compound which is quite strong and effective. Unless you get into refinishing on a large scale, though, I think you'll be just as happy using regular household bleach.

All the old finish and accumulated grime must be removed from an antique before bleaching. Small sections of old varnish or greasy spots will keep the bleach from penetrating at those points, and you could end up with a polka dot effect.

Once the antique is stripped and cleaned you need to sand it well to open the pores. Outdoors or in a well-ventilated room, brush or pour a generous amount of bleach onto the wood. Reapply more bleach approximately every half hour to keep the wood wet. Plan on using about a quart of bleach for the average 24 in. × 24 in. table. A softwood will probably respond quickly to the chemicals in the bleach while a hardwood may be far more stubborn. I've found I can speed up and intensify the action of the bleach by working in the sun. It seems to work more effectively.

The only caution here is to wear rubber gloves and old clothes. You're almost bound to splash some bleach on your clothes and it will remove every bit of color from the fabric!

Once you feel the bleach has lightened the wood as much as it is going to, rinse the area well with water. If you're not satisfied with the removal of the stain you could then try flowing on some household ammonia. Allow that to work a few minutes then rinse well.

Don't be discouraged if some part of the stain remains after all that. Some stains of long-standing will not give way completely, regardless of how long you work at them or what you put on them.

All that water you've used will have raised the grain of the wood and roughened it, so you're going to have to sand the piece again to get the satin-smooth finish you want.

SANDING TECHNIQUES

Many times the success or failure of a refinishing job is determined by the thoroughness of the sanding that preceded the final finish. Toward that end, I'll pass along some tips that may help you "smooth the way" in this delightful hobby of antique refinishing:

- Avoid rotary-disc and belt sanders. They remove too much material too fast and can leave scars on the wood.
- Avoid the very coarse grades of sandpaper. Use the medium grades for rough jobs such as paint and varnish removal and work up to the very fine grades for the final smoothing.
- Use a very fine grade of steel wool to rub down your final coat of oil or varnish.
- Sanding blocks are great for hand-sanding, especially the flexible ones.
- Paper-backed sandpaper can be made more flexible by pulling it, paper side down, over the edge of a table.
- Clean clogged sandpaper by tapping it against the floor or by raking a stiff brush across its surface.
- A fine grade of emery cloth is economical to use, since its backing lasts much longer than that of paper-backed sandpaper.
- Pumice blocks wear away quickly (and smell awful!) but

they are excellent to use on elaborate turnings.

- Cut emery cloth into 1-inch-wide strips and use them see-saw fashion to sand elaborate turnings.
- Steel wool twisted around a string makes an excellent sanding tool for deep slits in turnings.

COLORING AND FINISHING WOOD

Years ago all furniture finishers applied stains and filler to bare wood, usually trying to get the deepest tones possible. They then followed these stains and fillers with multiple coats of shellac. As a result, they obscured much of the natural graining and beauty of the wood. Today's theories, though, are to color and preserve the wood while retaining as much of the natural graining as possible.

When people ask what kind of stain I used on an antique many are surprised at my answer: "I didn't use a stain. I used a penetrating colored oil." This easy-to-use product is the choice of most finishers of antique furniture today. This type of oil is manufactured by several firms, and is usually sold as Danish oil finish. It is a clear, light oil which has several uses and is ideal for working with antiques.

The wood in much antique furniture is quite dry and brittle. It needs some deep lubrication, not only to bring back the wood's natural beauty but also to forestall future cracking and splitting. Danish oil finish does just that, soaking into the pores of the wood and helping to stabilize the fibers against future swelling, warping, and shrinking. As it dries in those fibers, the oil actually makes the *wood* itself about 25 percent harder than it was previously. Any antique so finished is less susceptible to all types of environmental damage than one finished in the traditional manner.

This oil comes in several colors, ranging from clear to a dark walnut tone. The refinisher can, therefore, color the wood of an antique in virtually any tone desired, without obscuring the grain in any way. I often mix the oils, too, to get special colors or to help me blend the different sections of an antique, the replacement parts with the old wood, and the different woods into one tone.

Pumice stone is one of the fastest and most efficient ways to clean old finish off elaborate turnings. It molds itself to the design and will cut away paint and old varnish from the deepest crevices.

Read and follow the specific manufacturer's directions for the product you purchase, but the basics are the same. Use either a brush or a rag to apply the oil to wood which has been sanded to finish smoothness. Wait about thirty minutes for the oil to penetrate the wood, but add more oil if the antique is so dry it absorbs the first coat immediately. Allow some moisture to remain on the surface of the wood. Wipe the wood dry with rags and then allow the finish to "cure" for an hour or so. Apply a second coat of oil, allowing it to penetrate the wood thoroughly. Wipe the wood absolutely dry after this second application of oil.

Wait twelve hours for the oil to dry and harden. Use this time to decide what type of final finish you want for the antique. If the piece will not receive hard wear or be subject to frequent spills of liquid, try this medium-protection finish. Repeat the oiling procedure of the day before, wiping dry between each coat. Give the antique a final polish by rubbing it down with a little oil on that ultrafine sandpaper known as wet-and-dry sandpaper. This paper is meant to be dampened with oil, and using it is a professional's trick. These multiple coats of oil and the final rubdown result in a lovely, lustrous finish that looks like old-fashioned hand rubbing. You can use it with confidence on hall trees, lamp tables, beds, or any other antique which receives only moderately hard use.

However, I would suggest you use a different finishing method for dining tables, children's furniture, chairs, or any antique subject to regular and hard use. In these cases, on the second day, buff the antique down with fine steel wool, dust well, and brush on a coat of satin-finish polyurethane varnish. For an even more durable and lustrous finish, buff again with steel wool after the first coat is dry and apply a second coat of polyurethane. This tough finish is virtually waterproof yet *still* has a beautiful, deep luster that is a joy to behold.

TOUCH-UP TRICKS

Granted, many times you must completely refinish an antique all the way from stripping through the final finish. You'd have no choice, for instance, if you found a lovely old cherry wood china cabinet that some Neanderthal had painted "Brite Silver" to accent his collection of 472 beer cans.

You don't need to ruin the patina of an antique, though, by stripping, sanding and refinishing just to remove a little minor damage. Many nicks and marks can be quite satisfactorily dispatched or diminished with some easy touch-up techniques.

The following techniques are simple to manage and will cover some of the most common minor problems with the finishes of those antiques we love. But don't go overboard and try to eliminate every dent and strain. An antique should have a *few* "beauty marks" to testify to its long and useful life!

MINOR SCRATCHES You can often remove a hairline scratch from a highly polished surface with fine steel wool and any lightweight oil, such as 3-In One or sewing machine oil. Just dip the pad of steel wool into the oil and *gently* rub the wood in the direction of the grain. This very mild abrasion will remove only the thinnest film from the finish, but it might work. If the scratch is still visible, try disguising it. Break a pecan, walnut, or brazil nut meat in half and rub the cut side along the scratch. The oil in these nut meats sometimes blends perfectly with antique finishes. Iodine often will do the same on mahogany. Apply it with a tiny brush— old lipstick or eyeliner brushes are perfect—or dip the end of a toothpick in the iodine and draw the tip along the scratch. Add a bit of alcohol to the iodine if it appears to be too dark for your mahogany. Regular wood stain or penetrating oils can be used, of course, as can paste shoe polish. Even a child's wax crayon can sometimes be used to match an offbeat color. Once the scratch is filled by any of these materials, rewax the entire surface of the antique with paste wax and buff to a sheen. The scratch should be virtually invisible.

SMALL DENTS A dent happens when wood fibers are compressed through pressure. To get rid of the dent you must decompress the fibers. Heat and steam will usually do the trick. Remove all wax and polish from the dented area with pain thinner or turpentine. Wipe away any excess solvent with a dry tissue. Fold a piece of cheesecloth or other soft, loosely woven fabric into a tiny pad, dampen it thoroughly with water, and place it over the dent. Allow the pad to remain on the dent for an hour or so, adding more water if the pad begins to dry out. Place a metal bottle cap, flat side down, on the damp pad directly over the dent. Set your household iron to "high" and rest it on the cap. The heat from the iron will be transferred through the bottle cap, will create steam from the wet pad, and should swell the dented fibers. Try again if the first attempt is not successful. Then rewax and polish.

GOUGES A gouge is deeper than a dent and can't be ignored. You can fill them with any of several commercial products made specifically for filling spaces in wood. These fillers are called by different trade names, but most have the word "dough," "filler," or "putty" somewhere in the name. Buy a filler in a shade as close to the finished color of the antique as possible. You can alter the filler's color somewhat by dabbing on some opaque stain.

Assuming you don't plan to refinish the entire antique, I would suggest *not* sanding the area around the gouge. Sanding removes the old finish as well as some of the old wood. You could end up with a light-colored area that is quite difficult to blend with the rest of the finish. Just push the filler material into the gouge and smooth it with your finger. This repair may be quite visible, since the filler material won't have the surrounding wood's grain. To camouflage the repair a bit do not fill the gouge completely with the filler material. Allow a ⅛-inch or so depression between the top of the filler and the surface of the wood. Once the filler is hard, begin filling in that depression with successive coats of polyurethane varnish. Use a cotton swab as an applicator. Brush a coat of the polyurethane in the depression, allow it to dry, and swab on another coat. Warning! This can take days. Once you've raised the level of the depression to that of the surrounding area, buff the patch lightly with fine steel wool and rewax the entire surface. All this is time-consuming but the resulting finish seems to have some depth to it and is usually less noticeable than the flat opaqueness of filler alone.

INK SPOTS The problem of trying to bleach ink spots out of bare wood is covered earlier in this chapter. When the ink spots are on the *top* of a finish you stand a pretty good chance of removing them *if* the old finish is quite hard and in good condition. Rub the spots out with powdered pumice mixed to the consistency of heavy cream with a light all-purpose household oil. Just dip a rag into the pumice and oil mixture and rub briskly with the grain. You may have to touch up the shellac or varnish because of this abrasion but you shouldn't have to recolor the wood.

CIGARETTE BURNS Cigarettes left burning on the top of a piece of furniture leave deep indentations, ones impossible to sand away. About the only option you have when faced with such damage is to scrape away the soft blackened wood with a sharp knife and then fill the resulting hole with wood filler. Use the method mentioned in the section on gouges in this chapter.

PRESERVING STENCILS Many antiques were originally decorated with delicate stencils, and it's always a good idea to preserve these if possible. I found a charming little high chair once which had a faint stencil design on the seat still visible through the old dark shellac. By using the following method I was able to save the design, renovate the high chair, and then surprise one of my daughters with it as a gift for her first baby.

You must use a very light hand to get the old shellac off the design. Scrape the shellac off with either a commercial scraper or a small knife. I think you have more control with a knife but that's a personal preference. Work in a good light, removing only a small amount of material at a time until you've cut through the shellac and seem to be right at the stencil. At that point put the scraper or knife away and begin working with fine steel wool and alcohol. Dab at the stencil carefully until the alcohol begins to dissolve the remaining shellac. If any of the stencil disappears with the shellac, stop immediately—you've gone far enough. Use the amalgamation technique to clean and renovate the rest of the antique, working *around* the stenciled area.

REMOVING DECALS   A couple of generations back it seemed the whole world acquired a bad case of "decalmania." Whenever the urge struck to decorate some existing piece of furniture, the answer often seemed to be, "Brighten it up with some decals!" As a result, we often find certain antiques, most frequently high chairs and kitchen chairs, embellished with those shiny renditions of yellow butterflies and blue Dutch windmills. About the only good thing we have to say today about these decals is that they were durable! You can remove them without damaging the wood underneath simply by soaking the decal in vinegar. They'll peel off with just a bit of encouragement from you and a blunt table knife.

FOGGY AND MILKY-LOOKING FINISHES   Moisture is one of the chief enemies of antique finishes. These blushes sometimes found on old pieces of furniture are caused by moisture penetrating the overall finish. You may have to try several different remedies before finding the one that will work on a particular antique. Start by removing all old wax and polish with turpentine. Occasionally this cleaning will remove the problem, but if it doesn't, try one or more of these remedies:

- Dip a pad of fine steel wool into linseed oil and rub it over the finish, moving always in the direction of the grain.
- Mix two parts paraffin oil and one part white shellac. Dip a

pad of fine steel wool in this mixture and rub with the grain.
- Mix linseed oil and turpentine half and half and rub the finish with this mixture, always with the grain.
- Sponge the finish with a mild vinegar and water mixture.

In every case, rub the piece of furniture completely dry with soft rags after the treatment, and rewax with a good paste wax.

WHITE RINGS   White rings on furniture are caused by moisture penetrating the area, usually from a wet glass or drippy potted plant. These rings usually don't reach down beyond the surface of the finish, so they're easy to remove. You don't need any special product, either. Any one of several home remedies is almost bound to work on any white ring you encounter. One word of caution, however—just to be on the safe side, try the remedy on an inconspicuous spot before you rub it on the white ring.

Here are several tried and true methods to eliminate white rings:
- Dip a soft rag into any light oil (cooking oil, sewing machine oil, petroleum jelly, furniture oil, etc.) then into cigarette ash or baking soda. Rub the ring gently.
- Rub the area gently with a half and half mixture of baking soda and toothpaste on a damp cloth.
- Dip a piece of fine steel wool into denatured alcohol and rub the area gently.
- Saturate a soft cloth with any good furniture wax and rub the area vigorously.

It shouldn't take you more than five minutes to remove the ring with any of these methods.

BLACK MARKS   Moisture can also cause ugly, permanent black marks if it is allowed to penetrate through the finish and into the wood itself.

Some black marks can be removed, or at least lessened, if you invest a little time and elbow grease. Using a medium-grade sandpaper, sand the mark until the surface is slightly roughened. This will open the pores of the wood to accept your bleach. Try to sand as little of the undamaged wood as possible. This may mean sanding across the grain on a circular mark, a real no-no in most instances, but it often can't be helped in this case.

Once you're down to the bare wood you can try bleaching the mark away, according to the directions in the section on bleaching, then refinish to match the surrounding finish.

Take heart if you can't get all the black marks out of your antique. Many are impossible to remove. A small amount of damage, if not too disfiguring, can actually be part of the charm of an antique, though, attesting to its years of usefulness.

STAINED MARBLE

Marble, which is limestone recrystallized under heat and pressure, has been treasured for statuary and fine architecture since classical Greece and Rome. Its slightly translucent surface, which reflects a degree of light, makes it a subtle and desirable complement to the opaqueness of wood. Add to that the fact that marble is hard, durable, and not readily damaged by extremes of heat or cold, and it is easy to understand why we still value it today.

Some of today's most cherished and valuable antiques are topped with marble. Yet, for all its durability, marble will absorb dirt and can stain if neglected. Unfortunately, the marble top of any antique whose wooden surface needs refinishing will probably need refinishing, too.

The first step in restoring marble is to give it a thorough cleaning. Begin by flooding the surface with hot water. Then scrub it with hot, sudsy, nonabrasive detergent, using a soft fiber brush or nylon scrubbing pad. Rinse well by flooding again with plenty of hot water. Wipe dry with a clean, soft rag. Repeat the cleaning step if you're not satisfied the marble is free of surface dirt. This washing won't remove imbedded stains, most of which are caused by long-standing contact with household liquids or rusty metal objects. You'll have to continue working with the marble to eliminate those.

Organic stains (caused by tea, coffee, tobacco, ink, etc.) can usually be removed with a bleach solution. Buy a small package of whiting from the paint store and a bottle of hydrogen peroxide from the drugstore. Mix the whiting and peroxide with a few drops of ammonia to form a thick paste. Apply this paste to the stain and cover it with a bowl to maintain the moisture. Allow to stand for several hours, then wash off the paste with clear water. Some stains of long duration may not give up easily, so you may have to repeat the operation several times.

Rust stains usually are brown or dark orange and they take their shape from the object that caused the stain. Use one of the commercial rust-removing compounds sold in hardware stores to remove rust stains from marble.

Once the marble is free of stains, wash it again with hot, sudsy detergent to remove all traces of the cleaning compounds. Although clear, the surface of the marble may be quite rough. Surprisingly, you can actually *sand* most of that roughness away. Flood the marble with water again and go over its surface with fine wet-and-dry sandpaper and lots of elbow grease.

You can use a chemical called tin oxide powder to help you get the gleaming polished surface that is part of the beauty of fine marble. Buy a package of it at your local chemistry supply house or university chemistry stock room. Lacking one of these in your town, you might ask your pharmacist to order it for you. Wet the marble again and polish it briskly with the tin oxide powder on a pad of soft cloth. Keep the marble wet and the pad moving. Apply water as often as needed to maintain a wet surface. Soon a distinct shine will appear on the marble. When you're satisfied with the polish, rinse the marble thoroughly and dry it with a soft cloth. Now, wax the marble with some clear paste wax to maintain that lovely sheen and protect it from future damage.

METAL FLOOR LAMPS

Most antique floor lamps were made of solid brass, plated brass, and/or iron. The lovely solid brass ones need only polishing with a good commercial brass polish to restore them to their original luster. And unless the plating has worn extremely thin, you can usually polish even a brass-plated lamp back to its former glowing beauty. Count yourself lucky if you find one of these lamps in good condition. Rewire any old lamp you find, *regardless* of its condition. New replacement wires, sockets, and plugs are cheap, and old frayed wiring can start fires. Don't take the chance.

Many years of polishing can take its toll on brass-plated lamps, leaving the brass as thin as morning mist in June. The base metal showing through thin brass is quite unattractive, but I've found one viable way to bring the sheen back. Simply buff on a thin coat of the gold leaf metallic wax described in Chapter 8. This wax gives a deep glow which is quite lovely, and it is the only practical method I know to refurbish a badly worn plated lamp.

Iron lamps are a different proposition. Most of them have been painted over and over, and the surfaces are chipped, layered, and in generally poor condition. Therefore, I suggest you strip all the old paint off any iron lamp you find.

Spray on a good quality satin black paint then. Spray satin black paint on any iron sections of brass lamps, too.

You'll have no problem finding and attaching shades for those lamps which have four upright candelabra-type sockets surrounding a central socket. Just get a large glass reflector from the hardware store and a silk lamp shade of a corresponding size from a department store. Drop the reflector into the cup which surrounds that central socket, then rest the silk shade on the reflector's upper rim.

Use metallic wax to restore the sheen to badly worn sections of plated brass on metal lamps. This wax is easy to apply and forms a deep luster which is quite attractive.

A bracket cap socket has been installed on this Art Nouveau iron bridge lamp. In the center of the picture is a shade adapter which will be screwed onto the socket. The reproduction glass shade will then be attached to the adapter with the three small set screws around the rim of the adapter.

You may find that the central socket is quite large, far too big for the base of any standard light bulb. These oversized sockets were made for light bulbs popular some fifty years ago but unavailable today. No problem. Just ask the clerk at the hardware store for a mogul converter socket. This is a porcelain socket which screws into the larger socket, reducing it to the size of modern light bulb bases.

You won't have that problem with the popular iron bridge lamps, but they will present other difficulties. First, many bridge lamps were not built with the sockets as an integral part of the design. All you'll find is a hole at the upper end of the upright iron column. To wire this lamp you'll need to go to a store which specializes in lamp parts or electrical supplies. Ask for a bracket cap socket. This is not usually a stock item and may have to be ordered unless you live in a very large city and have access to a large lamp store.

A bracket cap socket has the round, dome-shaped cap that comes on all standard lamp sockets. The bracket cap socket will have a double bracket and a butterfly thumb screw, attached to the smaller end of the socket, the end the wires go in. Align the bracket's two sides around the hole at the upper end of the lamp. Place the thumbscrew through the bracket and the hole, and then tighten securely to the lamp column. Using about 12 feet of lamp wire, wire a standard socket, discarding its cap, using instead the one you've just attached to the iron lamp.

After you've wired the socket, thread 5 feet or so of wire either through the lamp column or along its side, depending upon the design of the lamp. This will give you about 6 feet of lamp wire extending from the base of the lamp to the outlet. If your outlets are spaced far apart, measure a longer piece of wire before wiring the socket.

The second problem you'll encounter with bridge lamps is in trying to fit a shade to that bare socket. Try a lamp shop for a shade holder, an adjustable brass ring which fits around the body of the socket. You tighten the ring with a set screw and then attach the lamp shade to the ring with three other set screws. The whole arrangement is quite secure.

Authentic antique glass shades are rare, but you can buy reproductions at lamp stores. They come in all sizes, shapes, colors, and prices.

₰ 7 ₰

REPLACING CHAIR SEATS

For every antique table, washstand or dresser I discover, I will find at least two chairs. They may be simple ones with charmingly re-strained lines, graceful ones with deep hand carving, or the enor-mously popular fanciful press-back style. Since chairs traditionally take the most abuse in any household, my finds are often in pretty bad condition. Stretchers are frequently broken. A hip rest and spindle may be missing. The chair may rock and roll like a kid trying out his first pair of stilts. And the finishes are sometimes unbelievable. All of these sad conditions can be remedied with just a little TLC and the information in the various chapters on repair-ing and refinishing.

Often unsalvageable, though, are the seats. Almost any uphol-stered, caned, leather, or pressed-fiber chair seat used for a few generations is going to be worn out. Only solid wood seats usually survive intact. This chapter will show you how to replace those frayed and ugly beasts with new seats to highlight the beauty of your refinished chairs.

This book cannot go into the intricacies of a complicated reup-holstering project. That is for professionals or for those who've had some personal instruction in the craft. So, I'd recommend that un-less you are in one of these categories, you take all chairs which have springs and webbing to an upholstery shop. The results will be worth the cost.

The vast majority of chairs I come upon, however, do not require this expense, since they are of much simpler construction. With a little practice you can do these reseating jobs, including recaning, yourself.

CANING

Few final touches enhance the beauty and value of a refinished antique chair more than a new woven cane seat. This sturdy and economical seat became popular in Europe around the middle of the seventeenth century and was in common use until the early nineteenth century. The earliest examples show a mesh much wider than that used today. As workers refined their techniques, later pieces were considerably finer and more closely woven. Furniture makers of the early 1800s had little use for this homely craft, however, preferring more elegant upholstered seats of brocade and velvets.

Toward the end of the nineteenth century a revival of interest in caning occurred. Consequently, many late Victorian and turn-of-the-century chairs we find today still bear remnants of their original cane seats. And remnants are usually all that *do* remain. Almost all of the chairs I find which were once caned had later been "refurbished" with a padded seat or one of pressed fiber, leather, or plywood. The evidence of having once been caned is always clear, though, and comes in two forms.

One type of chair has a deep groove cut into the surface of the seat framework. The groove is sometimes filled with old spline left from previous caning. This type of chair once held a seat of precaned webbing and you can replace it easily and quickly.

The other type of chair has a series of holes drilled through the seat framework indicating that it held a hand-caned seat at one time. With some work you can restore this seat to its original condition.

Precaned webbing is just as attractive as hand-caned, although the latter is more time-consuming to install. Both methods are included here in case you come upon a gem of an old chair that cries for a new hand-caned seat.

The cane you'll use comes from halfway around the world. This honey-colored fiber is cut from the outside bark of rattan, a tropical vine found primarily in China, India, and Sri Lanka. It is peeled off the green vine and cut into different widths, ranging from a miniscule 2-millimeter strand to a sturdy 6-millimeter band. Each has a specific use in some form of caning or rattan work.

You can buy caning materials at many large craft shops in metropolitan areas. Also, almost every handicraft magazine and many women's magazines carry ads offering kits. Each kit contains enough material to cane one chair, the necessary tools, and complete instructions. Almost anyone who is adept with his or her hands can do a credible job with one of these kits. Then, with the confidence of experience behind you, consider buying your material in bulk. See the section on resources for a list of these mail order suppliers. Expect the price you pay for this bulk cane to be about one-third to one-half of the price of the kits. At this writing, for instance, a cane-webbing kit costs about $12. The same material bought from a mail order supplier costs about $4.

HAND-CANING Before you begin recaning, remove any old cane that remains on the chair. Use shears to cut away as much as you can. Then use an ice pick or awl for cleaning out the holes. Make sure each hole is completely free of old cane, splinters, globs of varnish, and other debris. In an extreme case you might want to drill out this debris, using a bit the diameter of the holes. Sand the area around the holes and refinish the chair as needed.

You must determine which size cane to buy. Cane comes in a variety of widths, each identified by name. Determine your needs by measuring both the distance between the holes, measured from center to center, and the diameter of the holes. The following measurements are pretty standard and will help you make the right choice.

IF DIAMETER OF HOLE IS:	AND DISTANCE BETWEEN HOLES IS:	ORDER THIS TYPE OF CANE:	WIDTH WILL BE:
1/8 in.	3/8 in.	Carriage or super fine	2 mm
3/16 in.	1/2 in.	Fine fine	2 1/4 mm
3/16 in.	5/8 in.	Fine	2 1/2 mm
1/4 in.	3/4 in.	Narrow medium	2 3/4 mm
1/4 in.	3/4 in.	or medium	3 mm
5/16 in.	7/8 in.	Common	3 1/2 mm

However, your chair may have been made by a free spirit who spaced the holes to suit his or her idea of craftsmanship. If so, just order cane by the hole *size,* choosing a slightly smaller width cane if you have to decide between two sizes. In addition to cane for the seat you will order binder cane, the wide strand that is woven around the edges of the finished seat to give it a neat, finished appearance. Binder cane is wider than seat cane and slightly smaller than the diameter of the holes.

If you elect to order your cane in bulk you will find that it comes in either 500- or 1000-foot hanks. The 500-foot hank is sufficient to weave two average 14 in. × 14 in. seats. If you have an option as to the length of the strands in the hank, order the longest length available. This means less tying off of the strands, and therefore, less work overall.

Cane is quite stiff when you buy it. To make it pliable, soak it in warm water for about two hours prior to caning. One way to do this is to fill a sink or large basin with water, dunk the cane in, and put some sort of a weight on top to keep the cane from floating. A heavy skillet works fine.

Some professional caners put a spoonful of glycerine in the soaking water. They say it keeps the cane damp longer once it is removed from the water.

It takes about six to eight hours to cane the average chair, once you get the hang of it. Soak one-fourth of the cane needed at a time. Take the first batch out after two hours and put another in. Working at average speed, this should just about come out right. If you soaked all the strands you needed at one time and took them all out at the end of two hours you would find that the last ones had dried out before you got around to using them. And leaving them in for eight hours would make them soggy.

If you find your bundle of cane contains strands of different lengths, separate them according to length and use the longest ones first. The first steps in caning are easier if you use longer strands, simply because you will have fewer knots to tie.

Keep a bowl of water handy and dip your hands in it from time to time. This helps keep the cane soft and pliable as you work.

STEP 1

Locate the center holes, front and rear, and insert a peg in each. Use either special caning pegs available from the cane supply house or golf tees.

STEP 2

Remove the rear peg and pull a strand of cane up through this hole from underneath. Allow about 4 to 6 inches of cane to hang below the framework of the seat, then peg the hole again. Remove the front peg and draw this piece of cane down through the front center hole. Do not pull too tight. Allow a little ease as the cane will tighten as it dries. Reinsert the front center peg.

Working toward the left, pull the cane up through the hole to the left of the front center peg and down through the hole to the left of the rear center peg. Keep the strands smooth, untwisted, and with the shiny side of the cane on top. Peg each hole as you work, removing the pegs (except the rear center one) when you proceed to the next hole. When you near the end of a strand, put it down through the last hole that will allow you 4 to 6 inches hanging down. Place a peg in that hole until you tie off the strand later.

Since most chair seats are wider at the front than at the rear there usually are more holes at the front than at the rear. To compensate, use one or two side holes near the rear corners to keep the last strands of cane parallel. Peg the last strand of cane on the left leaving 4 to 6 inches of cane hanging down.

You may notice that your chair has corner holes slightly larger than the other holes. Do not use these until you get to Step 8.

After the left-hand side is finished, begin the right-hand side. Pull a strand of cane up through the hole just to the right of the rear center peg, peg it, pull the cane down through the hole just to the right of the front center hole, and continue as you did on the left side.

STEP 3

Working from side to side, cane horizontally just as you did from rear to front. Start at either the top or the bottom of the chair. It makes no real difference.

STEP 4

Repeat Step 2, pulling strands of cane from rear to front on top of the ones woven in Steps 2 and 3. Keep these strands slightly to one side of the first row of back and forth strands worked in Step 2.

STEP 5

Begin weaving the strands from side to side again, this time weaving over and under the back and forth strands. Start from the last hole on the right at the rear. Weave the first from right to left *over* the strands of Step 4 and *under* the strands of Step 2. When you return the cane from left to right, weave *under* the strands of Step 2 and *over* the strands of Step 4. Peg each hole as you work until you return the cane on the next row.

STEP 6

Go over the entire seat, aligning the strands, making sure they are in neat pairs from side to side and back and forth. The space between the holes in the cane formed by the weaving pattern should be open and even.

STEP 7

By now you have quite a few pegs sticking in the holes, so it's time to begin tying off a few. To tie off, work from the underside, rewetting the cane if necessary. Grasp one of the loose ends of cane and weave it over and under one of the woven strands that pass from hole to hole. Make a simple knot and pull as tight as you can. As the cane dries it will shrink slightly and the knots will become quite rigid.

STEP 8

You now begin the diagonal weaving. Start in the rear right-hand corner, using that reserved hole mentioned in Step 2. Peg the strand of cane and weave toward the opposite front left-hand corner, weaving over the vertical strands and under the horizontal strands. Remember you are weaving over and under *pairs* of strands at this point. Complete half the seat, then go back, peg another strand of cane, and weave the other half.

STEP 9

Repeat Step 8, beginning this time in the rear left-hand corner. This time you will weave under the vertical strands and over the horizontal strands.

STEP 10

Tie off all remaining tag ends now as you did in Step 7.

STEP 11

Cut your binder cane 8 to 10 inches longer than the perimeter of the caned seat. Bring the binder up through the rear center hole, leaving 4 inches hanging below the framework, and peg it. Lay the binder around the perimeter of the seat over the holes. Take a long strand of the seat cane and bring it up the hole to the right of the rear center hole, over the binder cane, and down the same hole. Keep the binder cane snug and continue around the seat, up a hole, over the binder, and down the same hole. Stop at the last hole to the left of the rear center hole. Push the remaining binder cane down the rear center hole. Tie off all ends—and the seat is finished!

Allow the cane to dry overnight at room temperature and you'll find that it firms up beautifully, giving your work a most professional look.

You may occasionally come upon an old chair that has only a few canes missing or broken but is in good condition otherwise. You can repair this chair yourself using the method described above. Just remove the broken canes and fill in with new cane, weaving into the old design and tying off on the underside with the existing cane.

If you are *really* living right you may even find a chair once in a while with the old cane intact but just a bit saggy and dirty. All you need to revive it is a bowl of warm, sudsy water and a brush. Scrub the cane gently until you're satisfied you've removed as much of the grime as possible. Let dry at room temperature overnight and you'll find that it will firm up very nicely for you.

Obviously, hand-caning is a labor of love, and you just may not have that much time to devote to one chair. There is a way around all this effort, though. You can cut a groove about ¼-inch-deep on the chair seat just outside the drilled holes and then use press caning to reseat the chair. I've done this with several chairs and the results are quite satisfying. It is impossible to tell, once it has been press-caned, that the chair was actually intended for hand-caning.

You must either have a router in your own home workshop or go to a custom woodworking shop to have this groove cut. You decide where you want the groove to be placed, and then make a template to guide the router around the chair seat in that pattern. Caution: Don't place the groove so close to the holes that you weaken the seat framework and take the chance of its breaking through. I've had good luck by placing the groove about an inch away from the holes.

Once the groove is cut, you then cane the chair as described below.

CANE WEBBING OR PRESS CANE Cane webbing or press cane is a cane "fabric" woven by machine in a design identical to that achieved by hand-caning. It is pressed into a groove in the chair framework and secured with glue and a length of wedge-shaped reed called spline.

Often old chairs have remnants of the spline from previous caning stuck in the groove. This old material must be completely removed before you refinish the chair and install new webbing.

With a chisel go all around the outside edge of the old spline, tapping the chisel with a hammer to break loose the old glue and varnish. Do the same on the inside edge of the spline. Pry up one end of the spline with a narrow screwdriver or a spline remover, the tool especially made for this purpose, and pull it out of the groove. You may have to run the screwdriver or spline remover underneath the spline to force it out of the groove. A white vinegar and water mixture will usually dissolve any stubborn dried glue that remains. The new spline will not fit properly unless the groove is completely clean of debris. Sand the edges of the groove to remove any gouges or rough spots and refinish the chair as needed.

Most cane webbing today comes with standard ½-inch holes.

Traditional seats for hand-caning can be converted to those for press-caning by cutting a groove outside the holes. Use a router and a template to assure a smooth, professional cut.

This pair of chairs illustrates the results of the procedure described in the chapter. The chair on the left has had a groove routed around the existing holes. The chair on the right, which was converted in the same manner, has been press-caned and is ready for use.

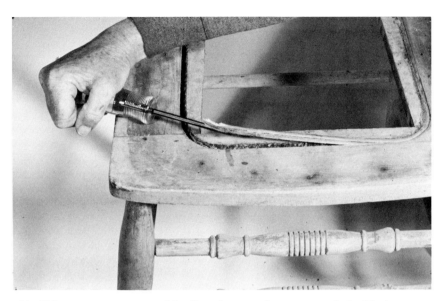

You'll have to remove any old spline that remains on your chair. Dig it out with a narrow screwdriver or a spline removing chisel. Be sure to scrape out all traces of the old cane and glue.

The only real decision you'll have to make is the amount to buy (assuming you don't use a kit) and the size of the spline.

Cane webbing is sold by the linear foot in widths of 12 inches, 14 inches, 16 inches, and so forth. You may buy as many linear feet as you want. To decide the amount you need for any specific chair, measure the deepest point of the chair seat from front to rear, groove to groove, and add 2 inches. Also measure the widest part of the seat from side to side, groove to groove, and add 2 inches. If a chair has a groove which is 10 inches deep at its deepest point and 12 inches wide at its widest point, it would require 1 foot (10 inches plus 2 inches) of 14-inch-wide (12 inches plus 2 inches) webbing.

The chair would also need 44 inches of spline, which is sold by the inch. Spline comes in different sizes to fit different-sized grooves. Measure the width of the groove of your chair and order accordingly. Every supplier has a chart in the catalog to help you decide upon the proper size spline. The important thing to remember is that the spline should fit easily in the groove, since two thicknesses of cane webbing must also go into that space. You should be able to drop it in and lift it out with your fingers.

Soak your webbing and spline in warm water for about two hours just before you install it on the chair. This will make the cane pliable enough to mold easily into the groove.

STEP 1

Take the webbing from the water, dry it enough to keep it from dripping, and then position it carefully on the chair, keeping the shiny side of the cane up. At least 1 inch of the webbing must extend past the groove on all sides. The holes should be lined up evenly from front to rear and side to side. Once in position, you can insure the cane doesn't slip out of alignment by clamping it to the chair's framework with a couple of small C clamps. This is not essential, though.

STEP 2

Once the webbing is in position, begin pushing it down into the groove with small wooden wedges. These wedges come with kits or may be ordered from bulk suppliers.

Start at the rear. Using one of the wedges, press the cane down into the groove. Tap the wedge firmly into place with a hammer and leave the wedge in the groove to hold the cane as you work.

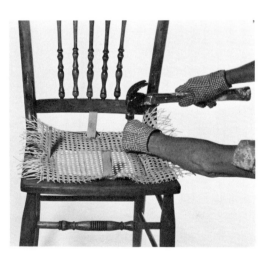

Refinish the chair and then begin the caning. Press the well-soaked cane into the groove, using wooden wedges to keep it in place as you work.

Repeat this procedure, tapping a wedge into place on both sides and in the front. Remove any clamps if you used them.

With a fifth wedge, go back and begin tapping the cane into the groove on the sides of the first four wedges. Continue until you have pressed the webbing into the groove all the way around. Remove the four wedges. The cane will stay in place now.

The spaces between the webbing should be straight both horizontally and vertically. The webbing will be slightly slack, but don't worry. It will tighten as it dries.

STEP 3

The grooves in some chairs have rounded corners; in others they are square. The two styles require slightly different treatments when cutting and applying the spline.

Since wet spline is pliable enough to mold along the rounded corners, it is cut in one continuous piece. Measure the distance around the groove, add about ¼-inch allowance, and cut the spline to this measurement. However, it can be difficult to bend spline neatly to fit a very sharp corner. It is better to cut four separate pieces when working with a chair of this design. Measure all sides, add ¼-inch allowance to *each* measurement, and cut the spline to fit.

Spline can be trimmed with a utility knife to fit an unusually small groove.

STEP 4

Pour a bead of good quality wood glue into the groove over the webbing. Beginning at the back, press the spline into the groove. Tap it into place with a wedge and hammer or a rubber mallet. Tap firmly but carefully so as not to crush the spline. If using one continuous piece of spline, join it at the rear center, trimming off any excess material. If working with separate pieces, press them into place and trim off excess material from each piece. Be sure the pieces butt securely against one another without any open space at the joints.

(*Left*) Lay a good bead of yellow woodworking glue into the groove. (*Right*) Press the spline into the groove, using a hammer and a wooden wedge.

STEP 5

Allow the cane to dry overnight at room temperature. It will be taut and beautiful in the morning.

Allow the completed caning to dry overnight. It will shrink slightly and become quite firm once dry.

STEP 6

With a razor blade, utility knife, or X-Acto knife trim off the fringe of cane that extends above the spline.

Trim off excess cane with a sharp knife. You can sand down any sharp bits of cane that remain with sandpaper or an emery board.

PADDED SEATS

Many of the chairs you find will have neither holes for hand-caning nor a groove for webbing. Yet there will be a large space in the seat indicating something was once there. That "something" might have been a padded seat. You can build these yourself using fabric to match your home's decor. The effect can be quite elegant.

I use two different methods to build padded seats for my antique chairs—depending upon the desired effect.

PERMANENT UPHOLSTERED SEATS This type of seat is neat and professional-looking and is quite easy to manage. Its big disadvantage is that the upholstery fabric is not removable, for cleaning or replacing, without dismantling the entire seat. Use a fabric that can be cleaned on the chair as you would with any piece of fine upholstered furniture. Use a piece of plywood or an old pressed wood seat as a base. The beauty of this wooden seat is not important; your main concern is that it is still in one piece and not cracking down the middle.

STEP 1

Place this seat on a sheet of newspaper and trace around it with a marking pen. Remove the seat and make two more outlines on the newspaper. The first should be 2 inches outside the original outline. The second should be ½ inch inside the original. The larger, outside line is your pattern to cut the upholstery fabric. The smaller, inside line becomes the pattern to cut a pad of foam rubber or polyester batting.

STEP 2

If you want your finished chair to look tidy from all angles, you may want to disguise the underside of the seat. To do this, cut a cover-up from sturdy brown wrapping paper using the pattern you made for the upholstery fabric. Center the seat on the paper, bottom side down, and fold the 2-inch allowance over onto the top of the seat, the part you will soon cover with upholstery fabric. Tape the paper in place securely with masking or duct tape. The bottom of the seat is covered, neat, and quite presentable, even from a worm's eye view.

STEP 3

Place the seat right side up now and dab a few spots of quick-setting glue such as contact cement onto it. The glue is not absolutely necessary but does help to hold the padding in place while you position the upholstery fabric.

STEP 4

Cut the padding the size of the smaller pattern, then place the padding onto the topside of the seat. Press it down firmly so the glue can grab hold.

STEP 5

Cut a piece of upholstery fabric the size of the larger pattern. Place the fabric, right side down, on a table and center the seat on it. The padding should touch the wrong side of the fabric. Fold one corner of fabric over the rear of the seat and secure it with a staple. I find that ¼-inch staples are perfect for this job. Pull the fabric taut and staple the opposite corner. In turn, staple the third and fourth corners, pulling the fabric taut each time. Then begin on the sides, left then right, top then bottom. It is important that you work from one corner to another as you staple, from one side to another, rather than circling the seat clockwise. This keeps the fabric centered and free of wrinkles. With all four corners and sides stapled you can begin working in the spaces between the staples, making tiny pleats to take up the extra fabric in the corners.

STEP 6

Turn the seat right side up and position it onto the chair. Tack it into place with the tiny nails called wire brads. I find that ⅞-inch ones work fine.

STEP 7

Cut a piece of the upholsterers' trim known as gimp 1 inch longer than the circumference of your chair seat. Place it right side down on a table and spread the underside with a thin layer of good quality fabric glue. Carefully, so as not to smear the glue onto the upholstery fabric, press the gimp over the brads. Start at the rear center, work around the seat, and end at the rear again. Trim off any excess gimp and press the cut edges together. Wipe off with a damp cloth any glue that oozes onto the fabric or chair.

REMOVABLE UPHOLSTERED SEATS   This method is quite a bit more trouble, but does result in a seat that is easily removed for cleaning or fabric replacement. As mentioned in the previous section, you will need an old fiber or thin wood seat to use as a base.

STEP 1

Cut a piece of 1 in. × 2 in. lumber to fit snugly inside the space which is in the seat framework. The best way I've found to assure a good fit is to mark the center sides of the space with a pencil and lay the board over those marks with the wider, 2-inch, side of the board parallel to the floor and flat against the seat framework. With a pencil, mark across the 1 in. × 2 in. board at exactly the places it crosses the framework. At the same time mark the framework at exactly the places the board crosses it. This will give you both guidelines for cutting the board and marks which show where the cut board fits into the framework of the chair.

Cut the board on the pencil marks without allowing any space for ease. This must be a very tight fit.

STEP 2

Once cut, spread good quality wood glue onto both cut surfaces of the board and onto the edges of the chair's framework between the pencil marks which indicate where you will insert the board.

STEP 3

Tap the board into place, clamp, and let the glue dry overnight.

STEP 4

Next day position the old seat which you will use as a base for your new one on the chair and tape it in place temporarily. Mark two spots on the seat about 6 inches apart and directly over the 1 in. × 2 in. board you glued in the night before. Drill holes completely through both the seat and the board at these two marks. Remove the tape and the old seat.

STEP 5

Follow steps 1 and 2 which were outlined in the instructions for permanent upholstered seats. At this point you will insert two 2-inch-long bolts through washers and stick them through the holes you drilled in the seat, pushing them through the brown paper bottom.

STEP 6

Follow Steps 3 through 5 in the section on permanent uphol-stered seats to cover the seat. The difference between this seat and the one in the section above is the two bolts protruding through the brown paper.

Align the seat on the chair, pushing the bolts through the holes you drilled in the 1 in. × 2 in. board. From below, put a wing nut onto each bolt and tighten it. You do not tack the seat to the chair or use gimp as a trim, since there are no tacks to cover.

This seat is easily removable just by loosening and removing the wing nuts.

PRESSED LEATHER AND FIBER SEATS

Sturdy pressed seats were popular with the turn-of-the-century chair makers, and the originals often remain on chairs we find today. Many are beyond saving but you can replace the tattered remains with handsome replicas in less than an hour.

Both pressed-fiber and leather seats come in sizes from 12 to 16 inches wide, and in round, rectangular, or bell shapes. A fanciful design is deeply embossed into the center of the seat, with the motifs ranging all the way from romantic valentine hearts to demonic fire-breathing monsters. You can order the seats by mail from several suppliers. See the list of mail order houses at the end of this book.

The seat you receive will be larger than you ordered. It will have a border of plain material several inches wide on all sides of the pressed design. This extra material allows you to trim the seat to any finished size to suit your own particular chair. If your chair still has its old pressed seat you can use that as a pattern to trim the new one to size. If the old seat is missing, make a pattern from paper, allowing at *least* 1 inch of overlap of the seat onto the chair's framework. You'll probably see holes in the wood where the original seat was nailed. This is also a guide to the finished size of your new seat.

Center the old seat or the paper pattern over the new pressed

This chair probably had a shaped veneered seat originally. An embossed fiber seat is an ideal replacement. The fiber seat is trimmed to fit the chair, then installed with flat-headed nails. Note that the hip rests will be added after the seat is nailed in place.

seat and draw around it with a pencil. The seat is then trimmed on this line with a utility knife or shears. After trimming, remove any pencil marks with an eraser, and sand the cut edges to smooth out any irregularities.

Leather seats are available in the natural tawny color or stained in one of several different shades. Fiber seats come unstained and can be finished to match the stain on the chair. Fiber absorbs stain quickly and it is easy to get a tone much deeper than you intended. So, when using a fiber seat, it is a good idea to test your wood stain on a scrap, a piece left over after trimming, for instance, to make sure you'll get the depth of color you want.

Position the trimmed seat on the chair and secure it with upholstery nails. Space the nails evenly around the edge of the seat. A rather flat-headed nail, instead of the hammered half-ball types sometimes used on old furniture, seems to look best.

If you're using a leather seat, you should have your chair completely refinished before the seat is installed. If using a fiber seat, hold off on the oiling and varnishing until after installation of the seat. Then do it all at once.

Both leather and fiber seats are tough. A little saddle soap once in a while on the leather ones and a quick wipe with a damp cloth on fiber is all that's necessary to keep them clean and in good condition.

REPLACEMENT VENEERED ROCKING CHAIR SEATS

One especially pretty style of late Victorian rocking chair had an elongated, S-shape, veneered seat which curved up in back and down in front. I've seen a few of these original seats in good condition but most are warped or broken, or have badly cracked veneer.

Replica seats are available, and installing one completely changes the appearance and usefulness of an otherwise unattractive chair. First remove the old seat by knocking the chair's seat framework apart to free the old seat. Lift it out, along with any slivers of wood that remain in the channels. Scrape out the old glue.

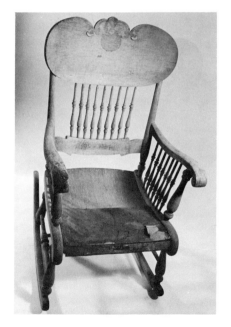

The seat on this charming antique rocking chair is beyond redemption. Former owners, however, had nailed on several layers of cardboard and plywood in an attempt to salvage it.

Molded replacement seats are available to restore a rocking chair of this type. The old seat is removed by knocking the seat framework apart. The new seat is trimmed to fit, then installed in the existing channels.

The replacement seat purposely will be a few inches too wide and too long, so trim it to the dimensions of the channel on your chair. Place a bead of glue inside both side channels. Insert the new seat into the channels, then clamp the whole thing overnight. After finishing, you'll have a lovely old rocking chair whose seat is good for another hundred years!

※ 8 ※

REPAIRING FRAMES AND MIRRORS

Many antique frames suffer from years of neglect. Often they are in fairly good structural condition but covered with generations of dust and grease. With this in mind, I'd suggest you give any frame a thorough cleaning before deciding if it requires refinishing.

Begin by removing all loose dust with a clean paintbrush or a soft old toothbrush. All old frames should be treated with great care, and when you wash one, use the gentlest possible cleaner. Two or three spoonsful of sudsy ammonia per pint of water should do it. Wring a cloth out in this mixture and rub gently over the frame.

Never get the frame dripping wet. Too much water can loosen old glue which holds moldings to the frame or dissolve exposed plaster trims. If the surface is still dull after treating it with ammonia and water it may be covered with a heavy coat of thick, dirty wax. This will nearly always disappear if you clean it with a cloth dampened with turpentine or paint thinner.

Sometimes even the best cleaning job will not brighten a tarnished or dull old frame enough to make it attractive. Yet you may not want to remove or cover the original finish. Try highlighting the moldings with one of the metallic waxes on the market.

METALLIC WAXES

Metallic waxes are a mixture of metallic powders and pigment suspended in a fine wax base (usually carnauba wax.) Sold in arts and crafts shops, they come in small tubes or tiny pots in a wide variety of tones, including gold leaf, silver, bronze, and a rainbow of colors.

The gold leaf wax is commonly used for highlighting. With your fingertip or a small cloth pad, rub a thin coat of wax evenly over the tops of all moldings on the frame. Use a gentle back and forth rubbing motion rather than long strokes, and be careful not to get the wax down into the base of the moldings. You will lose this highlighting effect if you extend the gold color beyond the very highest parts of the moldings. Then buff to a deep luster with a soft cloth.

To brighten an entire frame which has some color but is just dull, select a wax as close to the original color as possible. With a little practice you can even mix colors. Dampen a small soft cloth pad with turpentine and apply a bit of wax to the pad's surface. Use the wax sparingly. You do not want to obscure the original finish, just refresh it. One added benefit of this wax treatment is that it will often color and touch up small nicks in the finish, saving you the time and trouble of a complete refinishing job.

Buff the wax coating to a soft sheen and you'll have a lovely, gleaming finish that belies the little work you put into reviving an old picture frame.

GOLD LEAF

Genuine gold leaf is valuable and often fragile, so you'll want to retain every bit that's left on an antique frame. Simply clean the frame as mentioned at the beginning of this chapter, then polish the gold leaf with a soft cloth. *Never* touch up bare or worn spots on old gold leaf with ordinary gold paint. An antique frame with worn gold leaf is far more valuable and beautiful than the same frame amateurishly repaired with cheap paint. You can brighten an old gold-leaf-covered frame, by rubbing a *very* thin layer of gold leaf metallic wax over the entire surface.

Worn gold leaf can, of course, be repaired by the time-honored method of applying new sheets of gold leaf to the frame. Gold leaf is 22-karat gold beaten to a thickness of less than one-quarter of one-thousandth of an inch. It is sold in small squares which have a thin paper backing. The repairer peels the backing off, revealing a gummed surface on the underside of the gold leaf. This gummed side is placed onto the frame and pressed into the molding with a small brush. The result is beautiful, since the frame is, quite literally, covered with the finest gold. No one has ever invented a more elegant way to finish a frame.

Metallic waxes can be used to highlight and brighten the molding of antique frames. Touch just the tops of the molding design with the wax and buff to a gleaming finish.

These sheets are so thin and wispy, though, that they really are too difficult for most of us to manage. In addition, the price of gold today has sent the cost of gold leaf into the stratosphere. If you have a truly heirloom quality gold-leaf-covered frame in need of repair I would simply find a professional to do the job.

If you have or find an old gold leaf frame that must have some small part of the molding reconstructed, as described on the following pages, buy the best quality *gold leaf paint* to gild the patch only. This paint contains karat gold and comes in miniature bottles. Apply it to the patch with a small artist's brush and the repair will have much of the same brilliance and durability of the original gilding. Depending upon the extent of the patch and the condition of the old gold leaf, you may then want to layer on a thin coat of metallic wax over the entire frame. This will help brighten the old gold leaf and blend the patch in with the original gilding.

REPLACING MISSING MOLDING

Someday you may come across an antique picture frame decorated with a fanciful carved trim where some of the pattern is broken or missing. Many people often pass these frames up, thinking nothing can be done to repair them. This isn't always the case, though. You can repair or replace many designs with just a bit of effort. And you do *not* have to know how to carve wood!

Almost all apparently carved decorations on wooden frames actually are molded from a substance called gesso. This is made from a mixture of plaster of Paris and water. Workers molded the original designs from a similar blend at the time the frame was built, then glued them onto the finished frame. You can essentially repeat the process today to repair broken moldings.

Often you may have to replace only a small section of an elaborate design, a petal knocked off a rose or one edge chipped from a fluted shell, for instance. The easiest way to do this is to mold the gesso with your fingers and shape it to fill out the missing part.

Begin by thoroughly cleaning the frame according to the directions at the beginning of this chapter. Brush white glue onto the raw broken section of the molding. Make a small amount of gesso by mixing two or three spoonsful of plaster of Paris with a few drops of yellow wood glue and enough water to make a soft, putty-like dough. (I like to add the glue to give stability.) Gesso dries quickly, so you must work with small amounts. Make several successive batches if you have to repair more than one or two small sections of molding. It just doesn't remain pliable long enough to handle more than that.

Roll this mixture around in the palm of your hand until you have a smooth ball. Pinch off enough to make the repair and press it onto the broken edge of the old molding. Quickly shape the gesso with your fingers to approximate the design of the missing part. Use an orange stick, the back of a spoon, a small screwdriver, a nail, or any other tool to help you mold the pattern. Don't worry about rough edges.

Allow the patch to dry overnight and then sand with fine sandpaper to further refine the design. You'll discover that gesso sands easily, and the patch will soon be as smooth as the rest of the molding. Spray on a thin coat of clear plastic or brush on a coat of

Many antique frames have decorative multiple borders. These borders are usually made of gesso, which sometimes cracks off with time, as illustrated by the damage on the lower right-hand edge of this frame.

The first step in replacing a narrow molding is to
remove all loose and badly damaged existing molding.

orange shellac or polyurethane. This will waterproof the raw gesso
and serve as a base for the final finish. Then finish to match the
rest of the frame. I've used this technique many times, and, carefully done, the patch blends surprisingly well with the original
molding.

With a little more work you can actually duplicate a large and/or
quite detailed design. This may be necessary if your frame has an
elaborate design on three corners, but the fourth is badly damaged
or completely missing. Sometimes the entire frame is covered with
an intricate design and you need to replace a few inches of it.
Many old frames, too, have one or more fancy borders separating
large flat or curved panels. These very thin gesso borders often
break off, especially at the corners and outer edges.

You would have an extremely hard time trying to reproduce
these detailed designs freehand, but you can make exact copies by
making a mold using portions of the intact design. To do this you
need a package of modeling clay from your arts and crafts store.
Buy the kind that stays soft even after exposure to the air. You can
reuse the same clay many times over.

Tear off a piece of the clay and knead it in your hands until it is
soft and pliable. Flatten it until the clay is about ½ inch thick and
long enough to cover the damaged section, plus a narrow shoulder.

Brush a thin dusting of flour onto an intact portion of the molding. The flour keeps the modeling clay from sticking to the frame.

Well-kneaded modeling clay is pressed over the floured section of the existing molding.

The modeling clay is allowed to set for a few minutes, then is carefully peeled off the frame. It then has the exact design of the existing molding in reverse. Gesso is spooned onto the strips of modeling clay.

The gesso is allowed to harden overnight. The modeling clay is then carefully pulled off the gesso. The larger casting in this photograph shows the gesso as it comes from the mold. It must then be trimmed to fit the channel of the frame, as shown in the smaller section of replacement molding on the left.

A bead of glue is placed in the frame's channel, and the replacement molding pressed into place. Small cracks and holes are filled with fresh gesso. Note that the new molding is already in place on one side of this corner as I prepare to insert it on the other side.

Select a portion of the intact design that matches the missing section and dust it with flour. Place the modeling clay over the design and press down firmly. Wait a few minutes, then carefully peel the clay away from the frame, trying not to distort the shape.

Mix a batch of gesso to about the consistency of whipped cream and spoon it into the mold. If you're duplicating a thin edging you'll just have to spread gesso along the mold. Don't worry if some runs off. Allow the gesso to dry overnight before carefully removing it from the mold. Trim away the excess dried gesso until the new part fits the broken or missing section of molding. You probably won't be able to make a perfect match, but small cavities can be filled later with thin gesso.

Brush a generous layer of glue onto the frame and press the replacement part in place. Tape or tie it to assure a good bond. Fill in any holes with that thin gesso and allow it to dry overnight. Sand rough spots and spray with clear plastic, shellac, or polyurethane. Finally, finish to match the rest of the frame or refinish the entire thing.

Large, dry replacement molded sections are usually easy to work with, since their bulk makes them quite solid. Thin, narrow borders are another matter. If they don't break coming off the mold they probably will when you press them onto the frame. It happens to all of us. I've never found a way to avoid this problem. Just line up the broken sections as best you can. Again, small cracks and holes can be filled with thin gesso. Once the replacement sections of molding are finished to match the original design the patches will blend almost imperceptibly into the old border.

REPAIRING SMALL CRACKS AND HOLES

Many frames constructed during the Victorian era were of a rough core wood with a complete overlay of thin, smooth gesso. Almost inevitably, the outside corners of square and rectangular frames will be worn and cracked, usually exposing the base wood. Most of the time, too, the glue that held the frames rigid has long since dried out and disappeared. The result is usually four pieces of

Once all the gesso and glue was dry I stained the replacement
molding a deep brown tone to blend with the existing
molding. I highlighted the tops of the design with gold leaf
metallic wax and then brightened the rest of the frame with
two harmonizing tones of metallic wax. The original glass
and picture were then put back into the frame. A few
pleasant hours of work had increased the value of this
auction buy many times over.

frame with space at each joint, the whole thing held together quite
tenuously by four tiny nails, one at each corner.

If your first inclination is to take those little nails out and start
fixing the frame from scratch, don't! It is very hard to put those
mitered joints back together. Just squirt a bit of glue into the space
at those corner joints, then tap the nails to drive them back into the
wood. Put the frame on a flat surface while the glue dries. And

Many old frames are constructed with a thin coat of gesso over a core of wood. This gesso is often chipped at the corners.

These chipped areas can be filled in with new gesso, then sanded smooth. Two coats of craft paint will then restore the frame to like-new brilliance.

This frame had corner trims which were removed before the damaged areas were repaired with gesso.

The trim was replaced after this frame had been repaired and repainted.

These frames were bought for twenty-five cents each at a flea market. With just a little work and paint they're now ready to display heirloom handiwork or a family's favorite photographs.

make sure the angles are square. You can do this even if you don't have a carpenter's square by using four sheets of paper as guides. The paper has perfect right angles at each corner so you place a corner of one sheet of paper under each corner of the frame. Line up the sides and you can't go wrong.

Once the glue has hardened the frame will be as steady and square as when new. Rebuild the worn corners by smoothing on a thin coat of gesso. Sand when dry and refinish the frame as you like.

At one time, one of the most common types of frame was the

oval. Most families seem to have had at least two hanging in the parlor. One held an uncompromising photograph of Mother in her Sunday best, high-collared and proper, and gazing due south. The other frame had the companion photograph of Father in his black suit and walrus mustache, the picture of Victorian dignity, and *he* was staring due north. I've always wondered if it was the photographers of that day or the subjects who insisted upon such grim poses.

Many of these oval frames were of gesso over cheap core wood. I've found them painted everything from bridal white to bordello red, but most often in a dull brown with a darker glaze to simulate wood grain.

When I refinish an antique I generally try to get as close to the original finish as possible. This imitation wood is one exception. I see no virtue in trying to reproduce or save such a dreary finish. I paint them in decorator colors or gold.

Most of these oval frames with gesso overlay have a hard finish which does not take a stain well, so you have to repaint them. But, you don't have to remove any old finish, just sand it smooth. However, the chances are good that you will find cracks and nicks in the thin gesso. That old plaster is quite fragile, and time does take its toll.

You may use either Spackle or gesso to fill those cracks and holes. Spackle is more expensive than gesso but it has the advantage of staying pliable in the can and ready for immediate use. I find it very convenient to have a can of Spackle on a shelf in my basement workshop. It only takes a few seconds to open the can, fill a small crack, and put the can back on the shelf. There's no waste and no mess to clean up.

Regardless of whether you use Spackle or gesso, fill all cracks and holes, sand smooth, and spray with a waterproof plastic finish or brush with shellac or polyurethane. You will then be ready to paint.

The repaired surface of your gesso-covered frame must be free of imperfections for any painted finish to be acceptable. Otherwise the tiny cracks and mends will show through the paint and detract from the overall effect. If the frame has suffered so from use and

This garage sale purchase showed evidence of a long life. Many cracks and chipped areas marred the gesso overlay.

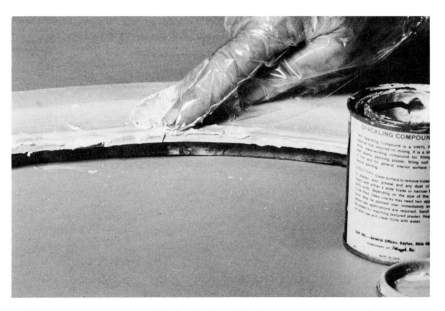

All damaged areas were filled with Spackle then sanded as smooth as was possible. Even so, the surface of the frame was not flawless enough to take a coat of regular paint satisfactorily.

The repaired frame was painted with an avocado-colored paint and antiqued with brown glaze. The result was an attractive deep forest green tone that blended well with the earth tones of my home. Once fitted with a new mirror it began another century of usefulness.

time that it is virtually impossible to make undetectable repairs you can still try to save it. This solution is certainly not one I would recommend for most antiques, and purists will undoubtedly cringe at the thought, but it is the best one I know. To salvage such a frame, paint it and then brush on a light coat of antiquing glaze. (Complete directions for the antiquing process are in Chapter 9.) The glaze tends to blend in the obvious repairs until they are almost unnoticeable. This frame will certainly not have the value of a lovely old rosewood or oak frame nor will it have the value of a gesso-covered frame which has been expertly and perfectly repaired. But it will be pretty and quite charming. Frankly, I would rather antique such a frame and so let it offer more years of pleasure in a home than throw it away.

Most of these oval frames had curved glass to protect those original photographs. Rarely will you find one with that glass intact. Some large retail glass companies provide replacement curved glass on order. If your local glass firm doesn't have this service, ask it to cut a piece of regular glass to fit. Your antique frame will then be a charming display for fine needlepoint, a bouquet of preserved flowers, or a family portrait. Or consider having a mirror cut to fit.

REPAIRING WOOD FRAMES

Wood frames are among the most beautiful of all antiques. You can refinish and repair them using the techniques described for furniture in Chapters 5 and 6 of this book.

MIRROR GLASS

Air pollution, time, and hard use combined take their toll on old mirrors. You will seldom find a really old mirror which is not discolored or damaged in some way. Many have deep scratches in the silvering, or large patches where the silver is missing.

I've found very few mirrors well over a hundred years old in top condition. The ones which have survived nearly always have a backing of heavy cardboard or thin wood. The latter seems to be most effective in guarding mirror silvering from damage. A wooden backing is also a good indicator of the age and quality of the entire mirror and its frame, too.

What happens if you should find a mirror whose silver is too badly damaged to use or sell in its current condition? Often I am asked if I can resilver such an old mirror. The answer has to be no.

The glue on this auction find had long since dried out, allowing the sections to separate. Its mirror, though of fine, thick beveled glass, was unusable because of badly damaged silvering.

Resilvering an antique mirror is an expensive process done with sophisticated equipment by experts. But they are few and far between. If you live in New York City or another large metropolitan area you probably can find such a company in the Yellow Pages. Most cities do not have glass companies who offer this service.

So, you, like me, will probably have two options when faced with an antique mirror whose silver is so badly damaged it is unusable. The first is to discard it and have a new mirror cut to fit. If you do so, be sure to ask for ¼-inch glass of the highest quality. The difference in price between a thin mirror and a fine one is small, but the difference in appearance is tremendous.

I have a new mirror installed in an old frame only when the damaged one is plain, flat glass. However, many antique mirrors were made of deeply beveled glass. This old glass is thicker and of far better quality than that available today. Also the beveling adds a great deal to its value. If such a mirror is in a good frame or piece of furniture do not replace it even if the silvering is virtually destroyed. With a little work and care you can restore it to its original luster.

While you will not be able to restore the *original* silvering you can *remove* it completely and salvage the beautiful glass. Then you place another mirror behind the old glass and have the benefit of a

The mirror was placed back side up on four bricks on the driveway. Note the deterioration of the silvering on the right side of the mirror.

Nitric acid is poured over the back of the mirror to dissolve the old silvering. Small children and pets must be kept away from the area when using nitric acid, as it is extremely caustic.

The nitric acid is swabbed around until the silvering begins to dissolve.

The dissolved silvering is washed off with running water from the garden hose.

The water is allowed to run until the glass and the area are completely free of any residual acid.

The frame was glued back together and refinished. A new mirror was cut to fit the frame and installed behind the now-clear beveled glass. The result is a lovely mirror with perfect reflecting qualities.

perfect reflection along with that deeply beveled glass.

Although removing old silvering is not difficult it does involve using nitric acid, an extremely caustic liquid available from large chemical supply houses or university chemical stock rooms. Nitric acid will cause severe burns if it touches the skin, so, as when using any potentially harmful chemical, you *must* keep small children and pets away from your work area. Plan to work outdoors, too, because nitric acid emits noxious fumes. And always wear industrial-quality rubber gloves and clothing that covers as much of the body as possible.

Place four bricks on your driveway or some other relatively level concrete surface and lay the mirror on them, silvering side up. Take a long stick and wrap rags around one end to make a swab. A broomstick works just fine. Tie the rags on securely. Pull the garden hose to that area, turn the water on, and direct the flow into the street. Wearing those heavy gloves, open the bottle of nitric acid and pour about a half-pint of the liquid over the silvered side of the glass. Immediately, cap the bottle and put it back in a safe place, preferably a box filled with vermiculite.

Let the acid work for a minute or so, then take the stick and carefully rub the silvering with the swabbed end. The silvering will begin to dissolve immediately. Keep rubbing until all the silvering is dissolved. This should take no more than five minutes. Add more nitric acid if every bit of the old silvering doesn't come off within five minutes.

Once it is all dissolved, take the hose and turn the running water onto the glass. The acid and dissolved silvering will rinse right off. Keep the water flowing on the mirror as you swab it away. Place the hose on the driveway to continue washing away the acid while you move the now-clear glass to a safe place. Go back and flush the entire area with the hose, allowing it to run for a few minutes until all traces of the acid are washed down the nearest street drain.

The glass will now be as clear as any window pane. Take it, along with the refinished frame, to the glass company and order a ⅛-inch-thick mirror cut the same size as the original mirror. Ask the glass cutter to install the new mirror *behind* the clear glass in the frame. Since the old glass and new mirror together are heavy, make sure the glass cutter installs adequate supports in the frame.

The results are nothing less than awe-inspiring. You will have a sparkling, blemish-free mirror that retains all the depth and beauty the antique mirror possessed many years ago. It will be far thicker than any modern mirror (which adds to the beauty) and, in addition, will still have that treasured beveled edge.

RENOVATING OLD TRUNKS

Renovating old trunks can be even more addictive than refinishing antiques in general. Once you restore one you'll be on the lookout for another . . . then another . . . then another. Perhaps this is because few antiques have so much charm, color, clear evidence of historical value, and modern usefulness as an old trunk.

I first became entranced with antique trunks in the early 1970s when my youngest daughter bought a big, flat-topped Wells Fargo-type trunk at the local Goodwill store. The trunk was covered with at least a century of grime, and we had no idea what lay beneath. She hauled it out onto our sunny deck and began scrubbing away. Two jumbo-sized boxes of soap-filled steel wool pads and a lot of rubbing later the original finish emerged. The trunk was covered with a smooth tin surface which was painted an astonishing deep burnt orange. It hardly seemed touched by a hundred years of wear.

The wooden slats were in fine condition and even the hardware worked like new, after a few shots of lubricating spray. The interior paper was long gone, of course, so she papered it with an ivory and rust print. She first took the trunk off to college, then moved it to a succession of apartments and homes. It now serves for out-of-season clothing storage and as a colorful accent in her rustic log home in Oregon.

Another daughter restored a barrel-topped trunk to use for blanket storage in her home in Denver. And I have a camel-backed one filled with fabric and sewing supplies in my spare bedroom. Each of these three trunks is now a part of the family. Even more than our antique furniture, these old trunks have ingratiated themselves into our lives. They're our heirlooms of the future.

Remember I warned you. Once you start refinishing old trunks you'll be hooked into a life long hobby that will bring you many hours of pleasure and an endless supply of gifts for family and friends. The trunks you give others, when you can't find space in your own home for another, will then become *their* treasures to pass on to succeeding generations.

Look for old trunks at auctions, flea markets, garage sales, and secondhand stores. Don't be discouraged by the abominable condition many of them are in. Short of complete disintegration, almost every antique trunk can be restored with enough love and care. The trunk on the cover of this book surfaced at a garage sale on a soggy spring day, and the owner almost apologized for charging me the few dollars I paid for it. The metal had been painted time and time again, and every peeling layer showed through at some place. The handles were missing and the brass stays had long since disappeared. The tin covering was completely rusted out at the lower edge. About the only things going for the old trunk were that it was basically sturdy and a small portion of the original lining remained. Fortunately, it was the section which held the decorative medallion that embellishes so many old trunk lids. If that old ugly duckling can be restored to beauty you can do the same with the next trunk you find!

As soon as you bring a trunk home open the lid and take a good whiff. Pretty musty, huh? That's because it was stored in some damp basement, airless attic, or smelly tack room for goodness knows how many years. You have to rid your trunk of that odor, so before you do anything else you must give it a good cleaning. You may find the tattered remains of an old paper or cloth lining clinging to the interior sides. Scrape this off, retaining any picture or medallion on the inner lid if it is at all salvageable. Vacuum thoroughly, using the crevice attachment tool to reach into corners. Once you have all the loose dirt and lining out, douse the interior of the trunk well with an insect spray such as Raid. Close the lid and allow the spray to work overnight. This will rid your trunk of any migrant silverfish, roaches, moths, earwigs, or other undesirable tenants. Do this fumigating outdoors to keep the little varmits from resettling in your closets.

The next day wash the entire trunk, inside and out, with your favorite cleaning solution. Use a commercial cleaner, pine oil, vinegar, or whatever. Finally, spray the interior of the trunk with a pleasantly scented room spray. You'll then have a clean, pest-free, and fresh-smelling trunk to renovate.

While some old trunks were made solely of leather, most had a rough wooden framework on which some sort of outer covering was fastened. This covering can be leather, canvas, tin, or cabinet wood. Each type of exterior will require a different restoration method.

Regardless of which kind of covering your trunk has, the first thing you do is turn it over. You may find a wooden bottom with small casters on each corner. Inspect the wood carefully. With luck the wood will be fairly solid. The bottom does not have to be in perfect condition to be usable, but it does have to be firm enough to hold the screws from the casters and to serve as a base for the trunk.

If still there, the casters may be rusty and balky. Clean them with a wire brush and hot, soapy water. Scrub away until you've removed the rust and the wheels roll easily. Spray the rollers with a good lubricant. If the original casters are missing you can replace them with reproductions. A couple of good suppliers are listed at the end of this book.

The best remedy for a trunk whose bottom is unsightly and riddled with holes is to make a new bottom from plywood. Remove any remaining casters first. Cut a new base from ¼-inch plywood using the same dimensions as the bottom of the trunk. Position this new base on the trunk and attach it with long screws at each corner. Make sure the screws go far enough into the corner posts to bite into firm wood. Sand the edges of the new base and either paint or stain it in a color that will blend with the final color tone of your trunk. Then reattach the old casters or install new ones.

I recommend repairing the base, if necessary, and getting casters in good working order before repairing any other section of the trunk for two reasons. First, you will be moving that trunk around quite a bit as you work on it and trunks are heavy. The smoothly rolling casters make the job much easier. Second, the casters raise the trunk a bit, leaving a half-inch or so between its bottom and the surface of the worktable. This allows you to paint, polish, or do whatever to the lower edge of the trunk without that edge being jammed against the worktable. Have you ever placed newspaper underneath a piece of furniture while you painted or varnished, only to discover the next day that the paper was firmly wedded to the bottom of the piece? That can't happen to your trunk if it is elevated a bit on casters.

Your next step will be to check the stays, those hinged supports which are attached to the sides of the trunk base and lid. They keep the lid from opening too far and tearing off its hinges. Often these stays are missing from an old trunk. If this is the case and the hinges are so firmly attached you don't want to remove them, I suggest that you install a temporary stay. Use a sturdy shoelace, piece of twine, or flexible wire, anything that will hold the lid on securely while you're working on the trunk. Don't put new stays in yet. They may be installed after the new lining is in, and that is one of the last parts of the renovation. If the original stays are still firmly attached just leave them on for now.

Next check the bolts or screws that secure the hinges to the back of the trunk. Many screws work loose from trunk hinges as the screw holes become enlarged with time and hard use. You have two options should you find bolts or screws loose or missing. The first is to remove any existing ones, separating the lid from the base. This allows you to work on the trunk in two sections. Many people prefer to work on a large trunk, especially, as two units instead of one. The only disadvantage occurs if you're painting the trunk. Since you paint the lid and base separately you'll have to re-assemble the trunk later on. The screws will not have been painted when you painted the lid and base so you'll have to touch them up, adding a step in the refinishing process. I think this extra step is worth the convenience of working on the trunk in two sections instead of one.

Your second option is to replace the old screws with new ones

One type of handle loop straddles the leather handle and is secured with brads driven through the loop and the handle. The original copper hardware shown here is a particularly fanciful example of this type of handle loop.

right at the beginning. Refer to Chapter 5 for this information. You will have to work on the trunk with the lid attached, but you do eliminate a little retouching at the end. The stays, whether temporary or permanent, must be firmly attached, though, if you go this route. Otherwise, even new screws can be jerked out of the wood should the top fall back suddenly.

Now take a look at the leather handles on the sides of the base. You'll rarely find a very old trunk with the original handles in good condition. Most are either missing, torn, or so brittle and misshapen that they're unusable. The original handles were attached to the trunk with metal handle loops. Remove and save your handle

loops, if they're still there, for later use. You can substitute reproduction ones if the old ones are missing.

These old metal handle loops are usually attached to the trunk
with short heavy nails. Use a tack hammer to lift the old nails and
release the loop from the body of the trunk. Place the slotted end
of the hammer under the handle loop and work it back and forth
until the nail is loosened and the handle loop can be pulled off.
Remove the remains of the old handle and fill in any resulting
holes. On a wooden or canvas trunk you would use wood putty to
fill the holes. Use liquid steel on a metal trunk. Do nothing to the
holes on leather trunks.

These handle loops fall into one of three designs. Some are made
to straddle the ends of a narrow handle which has holes cut into
the leather near the ends. A sharp spike on the inside of the loop is
driven through the hole and into the body of the trunk. This anchors the handle. A second type of loop uses the same type of

Another type of handle loop encloses the ends of the handle as shown here.
This, too, is original hardware.

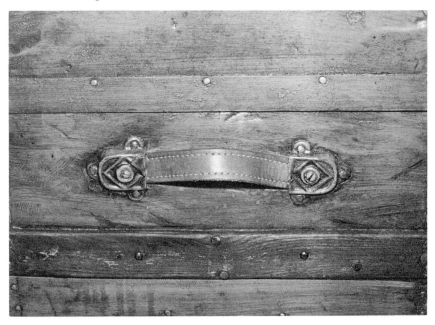

leather handle but instead of straddling that handle, the loop encloses the ends. This type of loop also has an inner spike which goes through the hole in the handle. The third type of loop is similar to the first mentioned except it does not have the inner spike. It is meant to be used with a handle whose ends flare out in a fan shape. The loop is placed just inside the flared section of the handle and so anchors it to the trunk

Replacement leather handles are available to fit any of these loops. Or you can make your own handle from a man's leather belt but only with the type of loop which encloses the ends of the handle. Otherwise, you would have those two raw cut edges showing.

You can replace virtually any other piece of hardware on an old trunk, too, including the big center lock, clamps, corner protectors, drawbolts, dowels, glides, casters, hinges, and stays. All these parts are available in reproductions identical to century-old styles. The manufacturers' catalogs also list embossed wood and metal ornaments which you might want to use to "fancy up" your trunk. Actually, one of the most justifiable uses for these ornaments is to cover unsightly damage. A pair of plump cupids or a bevy of patriotic stars are great for disguising holes. A horizontal spray of bows and roses is a fine solution to a deep scratch, and at the same time adds a romantic touch of Victorian beauty to an old trunk. The brass ornaments are attached with tiny brass nails and may be installed at almost any stage of a trunk's renovation. The wooden ornaments are usually glued on before the trunk is oiled or painted.

All the above replacement parts may be ordered from the suppliers listed at the end of this book.

The wooden bands or stays which encircle many old trunks may be so badly damaged you can't repair them. The solution is to buy a wooden slat of a comparable wood at your lumber dealer. If the bands on your trunk are not a standard size ask the shop carpenter to plane and trim the slat to your requirements. This is a simple operation and you may not be charged for it if you're a regular customer.

You'll need to distress this new wood with a hammer, deep and irregular sanding, or some other aging process. Otherwise, even

This old trunk was lacking its large lock when it was found at a Salvation Army thrift shop. This picture was taken after the top section of a replacement lock had been installed and as the lower section of the lock was being adjusted for correct placement. Note that the hardware is installed after the base color is painted on the trunk but before the antiquing glaze is applied.

though you finish it the same as the rest of the wood on the trunk, the new piece will look just that, new.

You can even replace the curved bands that fit across the tops of many camel-backed trunks by using a jig to shape the slat, as described in Chapter 5. An easier method for the simple shape of a trunk top is to make a rudimentary jig of six- or eight-penny nails and scrap lumber.

On paper, draw the arc you wish the slat to assume. Transfer this design to scrap wood. Hammer the nails on either side of the drawn line. Soak the slat at least an hour or two, then force it into the channel between the two lines of nails. Allow to dry overnight. Once dry, the band will hold the new shape well enough for you to nail it to the trunk lid.

LEATHER TRUNKS

Leather in reasonably good condition is quite simple to renovate. Clean the leather thoroughly with saddle soap and allow it to dry. Rub on a generous coating of a silicone waterproofing liquid, then polish the leather to a soft gleam.

Most old leather trunks had heavy leather bindings around the outer edges. If only small sections of this binding are loose you can repair them yourself. Work contact cement between the binding and the body of the trunk and let it dry under pressure. If whole sections are badly torn or missing you'll have to rely on your shoe repair shop for help. The repairer can replace torn or missing sections with comparable leather and stitch them in a pattern that closely resembles the original stitching.

Some of the leather which formed the body of these old trunks was quite thin, since it was applied over a sturdy wooden base. Time, sun, rain, and abuse have played havoc with much of this glove-thin leather, and some of these trunks are not salvageable as leather trunks. If the trunk as such is unsalvageable, cut all the leather off and renovate the wooden base underneath. This base, although made of inexpensive wood, may have acquired a lovely patina. In such a case, refinish the trunk as described in the following section on wooden trunks.

If you come upon a leather-covered trunk, however, where only one or two small sections of the leather covering are in bad shape you *can* replace those sections. Using an X-Acto knife, cut away the damaged leather at the nearest joining, be it the edge binding, underneath a strap, or under a wooden slat. Make an exact pattern of the area from which you removed the damaged leather and buy some leather of a similar color and origin from your shoe repair shop or leather crafts store. Cut a new piece to fit. Brush a coat of contact cement onto the wooden base and carefully fit the new leather piece into place. Press with your fingers then allow it to dry overnight. You'll undoubtedly have to dye the new leather to match the old. You can use commercial shoe dye or shoe polish. Just experiment on a scrap of the leather until you get a color close to the old leather. Then polish the entire trunk with a protective finish.

WOODEN TRUNKS

Renovating an antique wooden trunk is similar to renovating a piece of antique wooden furniture. First check to see if all joints, slats, bands, and corners are solid. Any which are not tight should be glued together and reinforced with recessed screws. Fill all holes and cracks with wood putty, then sand the trunk thoroughly. Polish the brass hardware with a good commercial polish and replace any missing hardware with reproductions. Oil and varnish the trunk as described in Chapter 6. The result will be a charming and distinctive accessory to complement your lovely antique furniture.

CANVAS TRUNKS

Many old storage trunks started life with a sturdy canvas covering glued to a wooden base. This canvas was certainly made to last. I've seen some very old canvas trunks whose coverings remained in remarkably good condition. If you should find an antique canvas trunk in good condition your first step in refinishing it will be to scrub the entire surface thoroughly with a fiber brush and your favorite cleaner. Don't be too harsh with the brushing, because you could easily damage any loose canvas. When the canvas is dry, check it over, inch by inch, for small tears, worn spots, and loose areas. Glue these down to the base with a fifty-fifty mixture of wood glue and water. Undiluted glue would leave a thick, shiny buildup on the canvas. Once the small damaged areas are repaired you will hardly notice them. And a few worn spots will just attest to the authenticity of your trunk.

Oil any exposed wood and polish the brass hardware. Finish the entire trunk with a coat of polyurethane varnish.

METAL TRUNKS

Rust is the biggest enemy of metal trunks. It is quite rare to find one whose bottom and lower edges are in near-perfect condition.

Turn your metal trunk over and examine the bottom. Is it covered with tin? Many old trunks were made with metal bottoms. If the bottom of your trunk is badly rusted, remove the casters and with tin snips cut the damaged metal to within an inch or so of the edge. Beneath the tin you will find a wooden base that may be in reasonably good condition. If so, use it as is. You should trim around the perimeter of the base, however, with some thin wooden stock to cover the sharp cut metal edges. Reattach the casters and you're in business.

If the wooden base is full of holes from decay or termites, construct a new plywood bottom as described earlier in this chapter.

On a badly damaged trunk the rust may have progressed past the bottom and started up the sides. This was the case with the trunk on the cover of this book. The metal was badly rusted about 1½ inches from the bottom. That portion obviously was beyond repair. My solution was to buy some wooden stock wide enough to cover the damage and then simply nail it over the rusted metal. If you repair a trunk in this way be sure to distress the new wood a bit before you install it. Sand the edges well to eliminate the sharp edges. Then beat the wood up a little with a hammer. Inflict enough "wear" on it that, once painted or stained, the new wood will blend imperceptibly with the original wooden bands of the trunk.

I also added metal clamps at each corner of the new wooden band. The design of the reproduction clamps was very close to the design of the clamps on the original bands. This, too, helped to blend the repair in with the rest of the trunk.

One day you may come upon an old metal trunk that just tugs at your heart. Once beautiful, it has fallen on hard times; the poor thing has rusted *all over*. My advice is turn and walk away. Unless you have access to metal putty, fiberglass filler, grinding machines, and the expertise to rebuild the damaged metal, you'll soon regret your decision to repair it. You'd spend far more money and effort trying to repair the trunk than it is worth.

You can *replace* damaged units of tin on an old metal trunk, however, by cutting away the old tin and nailing in new pieces. Plain, smooth tin can probably be found at a local sheet metal shop. Embossed tin, the kind used for trim on many old metal trunks, is available from one of the suppliers listed at the end of this book.

Use liquid steel to fill in any tiny holes in trunk metal or to bridge the spaces between old tin and replacement sections.

You may want to paint your tin trunk, especially if you replace any damaged tin or add a new wooden band. This results in an attractive, colorful storage piece which can be an asset to any home. You'll be happiest with your painted metal trunk if you use the antiquing process described below.

THE ANTIQUED FINISH

My mother had some words of wisdom which she impressed on me each spring when she called the painters in to refurbish the walls in our home. Without fail, she intoned, "Paint can hide a multitude of sins." Well, she was referring to walls, but the same homily certainly applies to old trunks, too. Now, I'm definitely not in favor of painting a wooden trunk that boasts a lovely, mellow patina. Even more of a sacrilege would be painting a leather or canvas trunk. Each of these trunks would lose much of its personality if covered with paint. Such blasphemy would be tantamount to painting a lovely old cherry wood dining table avocado green to match the leaf pattern in the draperies!

However, I certainly agree that painted trunks *do* have their place in the scheme of things. I have no objection to painting a metal trunk which has absolutely no distinguishing facets on the tin covering. Even some wooden trunks are improved with paint if they're made of ugly, mismatched boards that no amount of TLC can enhance. And painted trunks are most attractive when given an antiqued finish. This section will give you the simple directions to "antique" an antique trunk.

Working out of doors, remove the old paint or varnish with a good paint stripper. When stripping furniture, you must get every speck of paint out of every pore; when stripping a trunk to be antiqued, just get *most* of the paint off. You're going to cover the trunk with more paint anyway, so a little color left on doesn't matter. Do try to eliminate any thick buildup of old paint, flaking paint, or loose areas, however.

Once it is relatively free of paint, sand the trunk well. Brush a coat of rust-inhibiting primer/conditioner on a metal trunk. If your trunk has wooden bands you may want to leave them their natural color to contrast with the painted sections. If so, cover the wood with paper and masking tape. Polish, then cover any hardware you plan to leave unpainted.

Antiquing is a two-step process. First paint on a base, then wipe a glaze over that base. You can buy antiquing kits or paint and glaze especially for this purpose. Since every paint store may not carry antiquing materials you may have to shop around. You are looking for a low-luster latex enamel which will take the glaze well, and a colored glaze especially made for this purpose. Don't settle for substitutes; you may not be happy with the results.

When you find a paint store that carries antiquing materials look at the color chart which illustrates the results of different shades of glaze over a variety of base colors. Don't be appalled by the bright colors of the base coat. These primary colors are subdued when used with the glaze. The attractive rust color of the trunk on the cover of this book began with a flaming orange base coat, more vivid than any Valencia in the supermarket. After a few minutes' glazing, however, it took on the very livable color you see illustrated, one which blends comfortably with the earth tones in my home.

Once the trunk is stripped and masked you're ready to begin. Brush on a coat of the base color, beginning with the bottom of the trunk. When you turn the trunk upright the casters will keep the bottom off the work table and allow the paint to dry without sticking. If you did not remove the top from the base as suggested earlier, you will have to prop it up to keep the upper and lower lips from touching as the base coat dries. Prop a board a few inches longer than the trunk is tall under the lid, making sure the board does not touch the front of the trunk. The extra length supports the top, preventing it from resting on the base.

Paint the outside of the top and the base, extending the paint a few inches to the inside at both lips. Paint the handle loops if you were able to save them. Allow the paint to dry overnight.

Many people like to decorate their antiqued trunks with hand-painted floral designs. If you're fortunate enough to possess this skill just be sure to paint the designs over the base coat and before the glaze is applied.

The next day remove any masking tape. If you leave the wood bands natural, brush some oil on them, as described in Chapter 6 to preserve the wood and give it an attractive color.

You're now ready for the glazing process. This glaze must be brushed on and then wiped off. If you are using a kit, read and follow the manufacturer's instructions. With some glazes, you paint the glaze on, then wipe immediately. With others, allow the glaze to set fifteen minutes or so before wiping. If you are using the first type, brush the glaze on in small sections. Otherwise the glaze becomes too thick before you can wipe it off. Test a section or two on the bottom of the trunk first. It will help you decide the correct length of time to leave the glaze on for the effect you want to achieve. Remember, the longer the glaze remains on the base coat the darker and more opaque it becomes.

Remove the protective masking tape and brush the glaze sparingly over all painted surfaces and *very* sparingly on unpainted wooden surfaces and hardware. Don't forget the inside of the lips.

Once the glaze has set the recommended time, go back and wipe it off with rags or crumpled paper towels. Gently wipe in smooth, even strokes from side to side. Do this carefully, since it is easy to eliminate the entire glazing step with too vigorous strokes.

The purpose of the glaze is to give that old, well-used appearance, so leave more of it in areas that would normally show the most wear. Think about the places furniture shows age most readily, the places it normally darkens with use. Most people get the best results when antiquing by leaving a thicker coat of glaze at the edges of the trunk and around the hardware. The glaze will naturally settle into dents and low spots. Allow it to stay there, since those areas would normally be dark on an old trunk.

Let the glaze dry overnight. If the color is too light or too bright just repeat the glazing step.

When the entire trunk is dry, attach the handle loops and handles. Use new brass screws with new reproduction hardware. Any screws will do if you've saved and painted the original loops, since you'll want to retouch the screws with paint and glaze anyway.

Replace the hinges if you separated the top from the base. Retouch the screws with paint and glaze.

Give the entire trunk—painted sections, natural wooden trim, and hardware—a coat of polyurethane varnish. Protect the leather handles from the varnish with foil or plastic wrap. Apply a second coat on any trunk destined for a child's room or for use as a coffee table.

INTERIOR TRAYS

Most old trunks had trays at one time. Occasionally you find one with the tray intact; often you don't. Use the tray if it's available. If it is missing, either discard the wooden tray supports from the inside of the trunk, if they're still there, and use the trunk without a tray or just build a new one.

Should you decide to use a tray you will need tray supports on both sides of the trunk. Discard the old ones if they do not essentially meet the measurements and description listed here. You'll need two pieces of wood stock approximately 1 in. × 1 in. and ¼ inch shorter in length than the interior front-to-rear measurement of the trunk. Drill two or three evenly spaced pilot holes in each support. Measure the depth of your tray and make a pencil line on each side of the trunk at the point you wish the tray to rest. This is the line you use to position the top of the tray support. Run a bead of wood glue on one long edge of one support. Place it against the side of the trunk with the upper edge against the pencil line. Using long thin screws, attach the tray support to the side of the trunk.

The screws must be long enough to go through the tray support and well into the wooden framework of the trunk, but not thick enough to split the support. Repeat for the other side.

THE LINING

Remove any temporary or permanent stays for this final step in your trunk's renovation. But brace the lid by resting it on a chair seat or other support to prevent the lid falling back and wrecking the hinges.

Almost all old trunks originally were lined with paper. As well as being the most authentic lining material, paper also is the least expensive and the easiest to install.

Buy a good quality prepasted wallpaper in a pattern you like. An allover small print is probably best for your first attempt because you won't have to worry about aligning stripes or matching large patterns. On the other hand, you can create charming borders by cutting striped paper lengthwise. A word of caution here. Do not buy hard-finished vinyl-coated paper if you plan to use a self border. I've had trouble with a border peeling off when I tried to glue it onto this slick paper.

Uncoated paper is best in this instance. Other than this, your main concern should be that both the color and pattern be compatible with the age of your trunk.

Wallpaper *can* be expensive if bought at its regular shelf price, so I watch for the "odds and ends" sales. These orphan rolls are useless to decorators and paper hangers, yet there's enough good paper in one roll to line two average-size trunks.

Working with the base of the trunk first, measure the sides from top to bottom and side to side. Add 2 inches to the side-to-side measurement. Add 5 inches to the top-to-bottom measurement if you plan to have a tray and only 1 inch if you do not.

Measure the back, bottom, and front of the base as one unit, since you can line all three sections with one long piece of paper. Do not add any extra width or length to this long piece.

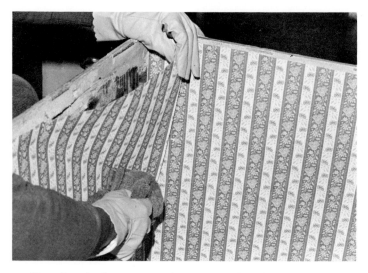

Note that the base coat and antiquing glaze have been
extended down an inch or two on the inside of the trunk.
This eliminates the possibility of any raw wood or metal
showing above the edge of the wallpaper.

Working now with the lid of the trunk, measure its sides. Add 2
inches to the side-to-side measurement and 1 inch to the top-to-
bottom measurement. Measure the back, top, and front as one unit.

Unroll the paper on the floor or on a large worktable. Keeping in
mind that you want to center any pattern or space stripes evenly,
transfer the measurements to the paper. Cut out the pieces with
sharp scissors.

Now cut 1-inch slits every 3 to 4 inches into both sides and the
bottoms of the two pieces cut for the sides of the base. Do not cut
any slits on the edges that will be at the top near the lip of the
trunk. Do not cut any slits in the long piece that will form the
base's back, bottom, and front. Repeat this process for the pieces
for the lid. Cut 1-inch slits in the side pieces every 3 to 4 inches
along the edges that will form the top and side edges. Do not cut
any slits on the edge placed nearest the lip. Do not cut any slits on
the long piece that will form the lid's back, top, and front.

Prepasted paper must be soaked in warm water to activate its
glue. Some paper must be soaked longer than others; carefully *read
the manufacturer's instructions on the paper's plastic covering or in-*

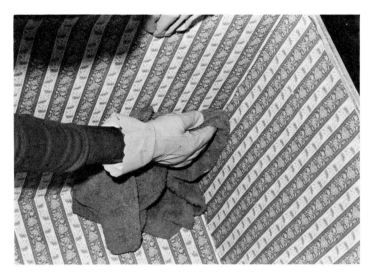

Use a cloth to smooth out the wallpaper, rubbing out any
bubbles or wrinkles.

sert. Put a few inches of warm water in the bathtub and lay one
base side piece in the water. Swish it around for the required number of seconds or minutes. Lift, drain quickly, and carry to the
trunk. Fit the piece in, allowing those slit edges to flare out onto the
back, bottom, and front, making a flange.

If using tray supports, press the paper up, around, and over the
support. Using a soft cloth, go over the paper, smoothing out any
wrinkles and bubbles. You will find you have 1 inch of paper
sticking out at each end of the supports. Trim about half of it away
and notch the rest to eliminate some of the bulk. With a table knife,
press this extra paper into the ⅛-inch space between the ends of
the support and the front and back of the trunk. Repeat to cover
the other side.

Next soak the long piece of paper, pressing it into place on the
trunk's back, bottom, and front. With your table knife, press the
paper under the ends of the tray supports. No raw wood should
show between the sides, the back, bottom, and front because of
those side flanges. Glue and staple the top edges if they won't stick
well. Repeat this process for the lid of the trunk.

Many old trunks had pictures or elaborate designs on the inside of the lids. These designs should be preserved whenever possible. Use an X-Acto knife to trim away any wallpaper that would cover such a design *before* you install it in the lid. Use the suggestions in Chapter 4 for reinforcing old labels if your picture is in poor condition.

Measure the distance around your trunk, add 1 inch, and cut two pieces of decorative braid to that measurement. Lay a good bead of glue on the upper edge of the base and the lower edge of the lid. Press the braid onto the glue, working the glue well into the fabric with your fingers. Cut another piece of braid long enough to go around the picture, then trim it out the same way, notching the braid at the corners of the picture to eliminate bulk. Instead of braid you can trim the edges with strips cut from the wallpaper.

Using the same techniques described above, line and cover your tray. If you feel the tray is too difficult to cover, considering the hand holes, lifts, and tiny compartments, paint the tray to blend with the lining paper's most dominant color. Or, make the tray, if you have to build a new one, of cedar and leave it unfinished. The moths will hate you!

Your final step in renovating this now-beautiful old trunk is to reattach the side stays. Attach the upper edge of the stay to the lid with a sturdy screw. Reproduction stays often come with brass brads but I'm a little distrustful of their ability to hold the stay securely. The wood framework in many antique trunks is sometimes less than solid from years of use and neglect. I'm always afraid those brads will pull out and the lid will fall back, damaging the hinges. So, I use screws which will get a good bite even into old wood.

Open the stay. With the lid upright at a right angle to the base, mark the logical spot to attach the lower half of the stay. Again, with a sturdy screw, attach the stay to the side of the trunk.

Now, sit back, admire your lovely, restored antique trunk, and give yourself a well-deserved pat on the back.

So You Want to
Own a Shop!

Sooner or later, almost everyone who loves antiques voices the wistful thought, "Wouldn't it be fun to own an antique shop?" The lure of working all day with those beautiful objects can be very strong. This chapter is written to give you some practical and proven ideas to use in case you ever succumb to the temptation.

I'll offer one strong word of advice, though, right up front. Before you open your own shop you should work for at least a few months in someone else's antique shop. The experience you gain there can be far more valuable than any general information in a book. Every town is different, and practices which would succeed famously in one town could fail miserably in another. A shop in a small town in Vermont will have to have a different personality, offer different services, and stock a different type of antique than one in downtown San Francisco. You'll be able to gauge best the needs of antique collectors in *your* town by working with a dealer there who has already learned the ropes.

TYPES OF SHOPS

Your first decision should be what kind of antique shop you want to open. Your choice runs from a full-scale business in commercially rented space to a part-time business in which you invest only a few hours a week.

COMMERCIALLY RENTED SPACE   This will be your choice if you're ready to give up your other work and spend some forty to fifty hours a week selling antiques.

Think long and hard before you decide just *where* to open this shop. Many businesspeople try to find a location where theirs will be the only department store, drugstore, hardware store, or whatever in the neighborhood. For many types of retailing, this is good business—but not with antiques! Competitive dealers find profits for all actually increase when they cluster their shops near one another.

The mystique of an antique shop is magnified many times over when it is located on a street or in a neighborhood with other antique dealers. The dealers in those areas usually go all out to preserve or create an atmosphere of old-fashioned charm on the shop facades and the street itself. They use flickering gas lanterns, striped awnings, stained-glass transoms over doorways, potted plants on the sidewalk, old English lettering on their signs, used-brick and barnwood exteriors, and anything else within reason to maintain the atmosphere of "days gone by."

Those of us who love antiques thrive on this relief from the concrete, plate glass, and steel that dominate most architecture today. So we find any excuse to visit and linger in such a neighborhood. The same urge usually isn't there for the lone antique shop incongruously squeezed in between a fifteen-story bank and Joe's Pizza Palace.

Antique collectors are inveterate browsers, prowling from one store to another, sometimes for days or weeks, before finally making a purchase. You can see this for yourself by taking up a post in a neighborhood where antique shops cluster. Stand on the sidewalk on a Saturday and watch the people weaving in and out of the shops, first on one side of the street and then on the other. Most will visit *every* shop in the neighborhood at least once before deciding to buy.

Therefore, each one of the shops in the area has a chance to sell to virtually every person who is seriously interested in buying. The lone shop on the other side of town just isn't in the same ball game.

In my small city most of the antique shops are located within the few blocks of a restored nineteenth-century section known as Old Town. Thirty-five miles away, the entire village of Niwot is, in essence, an antique lover's haven. An eighty-four-square-mile area in the Catskills resort area of New York contains over one hundred thriving antique shops. Royal Street in New Orleans contains dozens of antique shops, big and little, elegant and musty. All of these are quite successful, largely because collectors *know* the areas by reputation and know they will have hundreds and thousands of antiques from which to choose there. I suggest you emulate their success when you open your shop. You will never suffer by having your competition next door!

We can't always dictate our circumstance in life, though, and you may not be within reasonable distance of such a cluster of antique shops. In that case, you must make your shop so desirable that people literally will drive miles out of their way to seek you out. You might offer the lowest prices in the county or have the largest selection of antiques or the most interesting collection. And don't skimp on highway signs pointing the way to your shop. A large sign inviting motorists to "Turn Here to Granny's Attic Antique Shoppe" will entice curious buyers in your direction.

Running an antique shop full-time gives you the greatest potential for high profit. It also requires the greatest amount of investment capital and the largest amount of your time, however.

Co-Op Shops Many antique dealers now use a co-op concept to get their wares before the public on a full-time basis while requiring them to work only a few hours a week. Several dealers share the rent and utility costs for a shop, and each has an equal amount of floor space to display antiques. They divide the number of hours the shop is open between them, and each takes a turn at "keeping the store." They usually agree to trade off days and hours with one another whenever it's advantageous to all concerned.

The biggest problem I've noticed with co-op shops is in trying to be fair about who works which days. Someone *has* to be there on Saturdays, yet most of us like to have weekends off to be with family or friends. The only really equitable way to handle this problem (unless one person in the group really wants to work Saturdays) is to assign days on a revolving basis. A person would work Thursday this week, for instance, Friday the next week, Saturday the next, and so on.

Each person is responsible for sweeping and dusting the shop on his or her working day. The partners have to meet regularly to discuss any problems, to handle repairs or major moving of the stock, and to do anything else that involves each one of them. If one partner drops out the others have to fill in with time and money until another suitable partner can be found.

One variation of the co-op shop is where one person pays the entire rental fee and acts as full-time manager and salesperson at the store. That person then subleases space to other dealers, charging them a proportionate amount of the rent and utilities. The manager usually reserves ample space for his or her own antiques as compensation for managing the store.

THE IN-HOME SHOP   You may want to turn your living and dining rooms, your lower floor, or your garage into an antique shop. Fine, but be sure to check the local zoning laws first. Some residential neighborhoods have very strict laws about in-home businesses. You may not be allowed *any* type of business which involves people coming to your home. Other areas will allow the business if you don't hang out a sign. Still others will allow the business and the sign as long as the sign is unobtrusive and the neighbors don't complain about too much traffic at your place.

If you are allowed the business but not the sign you will just have to attract customers through word-of-mouth recommendation. Many dealers who operate this way don't keep regular business hours. Known as "attic dealers," they are at home to their customers by appointment only. While operating an antique business as an attic dealer is fine for a part-time business, it naturally is seldom as profitable as managing a shop full-time. However, many of us who started working with antiques as a hobby used this method to "test the water" before we went into the business on a larger scale. Many successful dealers who now manage large shops in town started as attic dealers.

The happy compromise between commercially rented space and an unadvertised attic shop is the full-time in-home shop with a sign out front. Who could ask for more? You have the chance to run a profitable business right from your own home, with none of the hassle of driving to work in bad weather and the trouble of maintaining two establishments. You make one mortgage or rent payment, pay one utility bill, one telephone bill, and can take a large portion of those bills off your income tax as legitimate business deductions. During slack times you can take care of household duties or work at refinishing stock for the shop. Women who run an in-home shop are there to supervise their children when the school bus unloads at 3:00 p.m.

One disadvantage of managing a full-time in-home shop is that it certainly can cause some disruption in the family routine. Children must be reasonably quiet while the shop is open and a portion of the house is off-limits for family activities. Converting the rooms into a shop will cost something, and those expenses must come out of the first profits. These alterations may have to be torn out later, at more expense, if you should decide to abandon your home enterprise and move the shop to commercial space.

UNDERSTANDING YOUR BUSINESS

Regardless of the type of shop you open, you will probably discover a distinct sales pattern evolves. Little serious antique shopping goes on during the heat of summer, but fall's crisp weather inspires people to get out and begin prowling the antique shops again. Your biggest sales time, therefore, will be from Labor Day until Christmas. For this reason, most dealers agree the best time to open a shop is in September.

Where Christmas is concerned, one friend of mine says, "Not many people buy large, expensive antiques for Christmas gifts. So I always stock a lot of framed prints, lamps, mirrors, china, colored glassware, and the like around the end of November. And I have gift certificates available for anyone who doesn't want to chance giving a church pew to his girl friend when what she really wanted was a player piano!"

Even during the balance of the year, from the end of the holiday buying season until Labor Day, you may notice a buying pattern among your customers. So to help with your own buying, you'll want to keep a running record that will show you, month by month, just what you sold throughout the year. If you find, for instance, that you sell more tables and chairs in May than any other month, you will know to increase your inventory of tables and chairs in late April and advertise them heavily for the next month.

I keep another record, too, that helps me increase my profits in this business. It is a detailed tally of each antique I buy to refinish. I note the purchase price, cost of refinishing materials, selling price, and profit. This record is kept in columns in a ledger so I can look down the sheets and tell at a glance, for instance, that my overall profit ratio on floor lamps and office chairs is higher than that on lamp tables and kitchen cabinets. This helps me know not to go overboard on buying lamp tables and kitchen cabinets because I make more money on lamps and office chairs.

ITEM	PURCHASE PRICE	REFINISHING COSTS	SELLING PRICE	PROFIT	
#212					
Rocking chair	$60	$38	$265	$167	63%
#213					
Round table	$200	$15	$425	$210	49.4%
#214					
Single bed	$65	$25	$195	$105	53.8%
#215					
Iron lamp	$8	$8	$95	$79	83.2%
#216					
Hoosier cabinet	$140	$35	$395	$220	55.7%
#217					
Small table	$40	$25	$125	$60	44%
#218					
Office chair	$17	$25	$195	$153	78.4%
#219					
Small desk	$50	$10	$195	$135	69.2%

This breakdown of costs and profits is in no way definitive, of course, since each antique costs me a different amount and some require much more refinishing than others. I might buy an office chair for $30 at auction, spend a full $45 on refinishing and hardware and still get the same price for it that I get for one where I have only $28 invested. But, *overall,* the cost breakdown helps me determine where my greatest profit lies.

PUBLICIZING YOUR BUSINESS

Your budget must include a substantial sum for advertising, promotion, and publicity. Many newcomers to retailing may cringe at the thought of paying perhaps thousands of dollars to advertise their businesses, especially when "everything is going out and nothing is coming in." Yet the fact remains, you must spend some money up front to attract the customers who will insure the success of your shop.

One of this country's most successful businessmen had a motto he consistently reiterated to the men and women who bought franchises from him. It was, "Early to bed and early to rise, and *advertise, advertise, advertise!*" I can't offer you any better advice.

Your grand opening is the first opportunity to make a big splash with the antique lovers of your community. Play this for all it is worth. Place display ads in your local papers announcing the date and flagging some special inducement for customers to visit the store. This might be a 10 percent discount on every item purchased the first day, a drawing for a free gift certificate, refreshments, flowers for the first twenty customers who visit the store, or something of the sort.

A feature story about the shop in the local newspaper on the same day the ad appears will triple the impact of that ad, and the story is *free.* To get that feature story, make an appointment, a couple of weeks in advance, with the editor at the newspaper who handles stories about new businesses. Call the local newspaper to get this person's name.

Pull out all the stops when you sit down across the desk from this person. Appear enthusiastic, knowledgeable, and interesting. Hand the editor a typed press release which gives all the details about you, your shop, and the grand opening. Include the five Ws of journalism (who, what, where, when, and why) in the release, and bring along a clear black and white glossy photograph of yourself taken at the shop. Ask a local advertising agency or a graduate journalism student to prepare the release and photograph if you don't have expertise in those fields. Ask the editor to send a reporter to the shop if at all possible to get more information for the story.

Make your shop as festive as possible on the day of the grand opening. Place flowers near the cash register and at several other locations throughout the showroom. Play soft but lively music and station yourself near the front door to greet each person who enters. If the area's zoning code allows, you might place some type of attention-getting device on the outside of the building. This could be twinkling lights on a pair of potted trees or anything else that is in good taste yet will attract the attention of passersby.

After the grand opening keep up a small but steady advertising campaign. Most antique shops do not run large, expensive display ads regularly. A small ad in the classified section under "Antiques" is usually enough, since most people who are searching for antiques will look there first. Change the ad weekly, featuring a half dozen or so different items each week. Make sure the name and address of your store is set either in boldface type or capital letters.

Join the local merchants' association to take advantage of any group advertising and promotion possibilities.

Try to get your name and the name of the store in the news section of the newspaper occasionally, too. Perhaps you could dress in turn-of-the-century clothing on the anniversary of your town's founding or some other local historical date. You could offer to take Polaroid pictures of each customer who visits the store dressed in period costume on that date. A local museum curator could judge the costumes, and you would give a prize for the one deemed most authentic. Arrange to display an especially valuable antique from the collection of a local person. Perhaps you could acquire an unusual antique to sell (possibly on consignment), one that would warrant a notice in the newspaper. Arrange for a well-known local historian to give a series of short talks at the shop. Perhaps he or she would give a walking tour of the town, beginning and ending at your shop. Be creative!

DECORATING YOUR SHOP

Some years ago antique shops were often formal emporiums that boasted imported crystal chandeliers above and oriental rugs below. The aloof salespeople in their restrained suits exuded all the conviviality of well-trained English butlers and schoolmarms. Many potential customers shied away from these miniature Versailles because they feared the prices would be as high as their knowledge of antiques was low. They didn't want to be embarrassed or made to feel like hayseeds.

At the other extreme were the dusty, jumbled "Old Curiosity Shoppes" that appealed to those who loved the thrill of searching for a treasure among all the junk.

Things have taken a distinct turn for the better. Today's successful antique shop is more likely to be a clean, warm, inviting store where the customer is welcomed in an atmosphere of down-home friendliness. Many store owners are "going natural" to reinforce this ambiance, covering their shop walls with quaintly patterned wallpaper and old barn siding. They're using hanging plants and priscilla curtains at the windows. They're aiming for a sense of rustic warmth that encourages customers to enter and linger. Unless you plan to deal in only the most expensive and rare antiques, I suggest your plan your store decor, too, to follow the popular "country" theme.

Your storefront windows can be an excellent silent "salesperson" and attract many customers if you decorate them well. One dealer in my town says he always features one or two real "crowd stoppers" in his front window. These might be an exceptionally lovely press-back rocking chair and chest of drawers or a charming child's high chair and cradle. These items are always in the middle price range and clearly marked so the price is visible to casual passersby. He wants people to know that he has quality merchandise at a fair price. He usually has a colorful stained-glass piece hanging in the window, too. A permanent fixture in his tall window is a potted tree that adds color and graceful lines to the featured arrangement. You'll find, as he does, that well-decorated windows are well worth the time they take to prepare.

A lot of people who come into your shop will be browsers. They simply love antiques and want to enjoy looking at them. Many, however, will be searching for a specific item to fill a specific need. They may need a set of six mahogany chairs to complement their Duncan Phyfe table, a walnut Eastlake commode to hold the stereo turntable in the living room, or a Victorian rosewood bed for a child's bedroom. You can help them envision *your* antiques filling those needs if you arrange your merchandise in room groupings rather than just line them up like boxes of cereal at the grocery store. This will help customers picture the way the antique would actually look in a home setting. You'll lose fewer sales because of that old "Gosh, I wish I knew how it would look with my furniture."

Go another step toward more sales by using accessories that dramatize the beauty and usefulness of the antiques. Place attractive floral or dried arrangements on some of the end tables and accent the charm of others with a few old books. Put some nice antique china and crystal on the shelves of a glass-fronted china cabinet. Hang some pretty hand-embroidered linens on the upper bar of washstands and drape a scarf or two over the hanging hooks of a hall tree. All of these small decorative touches will make the individual antique more appealing as well as add color and pizzazz to the entire shop. Few things are as dull as a shop filled with brown furniture and no bright colorful touches.

About once a week get to work early enough to rearrange most of the furniture. Switch groupings around so repeat customers don't see the same old arrangements every time they stop in. Sometimes an antique will look completely different in one setting than it does in another. This is one of the easiest ways to increase both interest in your stock, and sales. After you've finished moving the furniture take another half hour or so to go over each piece with some good furniture polish. This one act, neglected by so many dealers, can go a long way toward increasing the desirability of your merchandise.

Plenty of good strong light is also necessary if customers are to see the beauty of the wood and the lovely lines of your stock. Track lights are useful to highlight walls, which may be too dark to show off your wares properly. Place several lamps, floor or table, throughout the store. Your customers will find their soft pools of golden light inviting, cheerful, and home-like.

Put a small radio in some unobtrusive spot and keep it tuned to a station which plays easy-listening music. Most customers feel uncomfortable when they walk into a silent shop. The normal reaction is to get out as quickly as possible.

I'll offer one last word of advice about the interior of your shop. Keep a few of those floor and table lamps lit at night. Many customers will come back during the day to inspect an antique they glimpsed while window shopping the night before.

STOCKING YOUR STORE

One of your biggest problems as the owner of an antique shop may be developing and maintaining a reliable source of stock. Your shop will be filled when you open, of course, but with any kind of luck, you'll begin selling quickly. Each piece you sell must soon be replaced with another or your shop will begin to look empty. This means you must have the time to find and refinish as necessary a continuous supply of antiques.

Most antique shops are open about eight hours a day, five days a week. Will those nonworking evenings and two days be enough for you to get out and scout around for new stock? They may not be if you're trying to handle every aspect of the business alone. You shouldn't have any trouble hitting a few carefully selected garage sales on Saturday mornings before you open the shop, but what about the antique and estate auctions on Saturday afternoons?

Assuming you hire part-time sales help so you can leave the shop occasionally for buying forays, will you have the time to refinish the antiques you do buy? Will you be willing to give up your free evening and Sunday hours for refinishing? This could quickly get to be a real drag. I know of one dealer who solved this problem by having her workshop in the back of her antique shop. Actually, it was almost a part of the selling floor, with just a waist-high barrier separating the two. She did a great deal of her refinishing and repairing there during business hours while keeping her eye on the door for customers. She did not do any stripping, sanding, or varnishing during the business hours because of the odor and noise.

This dealer managed to do an incredible amount of work on her antiques by utilizing slow hours in the shop. This meant she could not wear dress clothes to work. Jeans, a sturdy shirt, and low shoes were the order of the day, but her customers didn't seem to mind the unconventional dress. In fact, her "regulars" actually looked forward to hanging over that barrier and chatting with her as she worked. They'd stop in just to see "what was cooking in the back room" and occasionally become so entranced with an antique in the works that they'd come back later to buy it. This dealer managed to keep her shop well stocked by combining these two facets of the business.

If you do not care to run your shop so casually, the solution might be to own your shop jointly with a partner who could share the buying, refinishing, and selling chores. A partner would also free you to make out-of-town buying trips to one of the several areas in the country where antiques are plentiful. At the time of this writing many dealers regularly take trucks to the Midwest and buy enough antiques to keep them in business for six months or more. Iowa seems to be a favorite spot, but some make wide-ranging forays that cover half the country. They attend country auctions, place "antiques-wanted" ads in small town newspapers, and buy from wholesalers in many states.

These wholesalers run ads in the antique industry trade papers. Dealers contact them and examine their stock. They determine if the prices are compatible with making a profit "back home." If so, a deal is made and the dealer loads up the truck for the trek home. These wholesalers are especially valuable to the dealer who lives in an area particularly devoid of antiques.

While the antique business is not so faddish as some, trends *do* develop, and the wise dealer keeps on top of them. It will do no good, for instance, to have a shop full of beautifully refinished formal mahogany Chippendale- and Hepplewhite-style furniture if

90 percent of the people in your area are buying casual, turn-of-the-century oak.

You should constantly research current information about your trade. You can keep up on *overall* trends in the antique business by reading the half dozen or so excellent trade journals on the market. To judge local tastes, though, you can hardly do better than to attend local antique auctions. You'll get dramatic and fast proof of just what is "hot" in your area. All you have to do is watch the temperature level of the bidding. Popular items will be bid up to high prices while the duds no one wants will go begging.

I attended an auction recently that aptly demonstrated this point. A set of four walnut chairs came up for bid. Now these were early Victorian style, in pretty good condition, and probably 125 years old. The auctioneer described them fully, extolled their virtues, and called for bids. Nothing happened. Finally, with some prodding he got an opening bid of $10 apiece. After a great deal of effort on his part he slowly worked that bid up to $35 apiece. And the bidding stuck there. These were nice chairs, and a generation ago here, or in other parts of the country now, they would have brought much higher bids. But most dealers who are buying for resale now in my area are not buying early Victorian walnut because so few customers call for it.

An hour or so later a set of four late Victorian press-back oak chairs came up. And all heck broke loose. You'd have thought those chairs were put together with gold screws! The bidding was fast and furious, with hands popping up all over the room. In seconds the dozen or more eager bidders had raised the bidding to $65 each for those chairs. The bidding slowed a bit then and finally stopped at $75 each. The reason? A set of four pretty press-back oak chairs in my town will bring $500 and up. The dealer who bought those chairs went home with a guaranteed future profit in his pocket.

Later on an attractive and sturdy buffet came up for bids. Again people sat on their hands. No one wanted it, and the auctioneer finally sold it for a paltry $85. Not long afterwards a china cabinet came up. It was in no better condition than the buffet and no less useful, but those same dealers and individuals who had vied so avidly for the press-back chairs started bidding furiously for it. The cabinet finally sold for $470. Now, what would all that tell the neophyte shop owner in my town? Put your money in press-back oak chairs and china cabinets, not walnut chairs and buffets. That's what the customers want and will buy.

Many successful dealers follow the "rule of three" when stocking their shops. They try to have three of any one type of item, china cabinets, for instance. One china cabinet will be priced to sell quite low. Another might have curved glass and claw feet and be priced in the middle range. The third will be a real bell-ringer with a beveled mirror, lovely carved trim, and stained-glass inserts, and with a correspondingly high price tag. This gives customers a good selection without overwhelming them with too many options. If you only had one china cabinet the customer might understandably think, "This is nice, but I really should shop around before I buy." By offering three cabinets in a range of styles and prices, you have a much better chance to make a sale before the customer leaves your shop.

Be cautious about investing in any antique, no matter how beautiful, that will not fit into the average home or apartment. A friend of mine fell into that trap and lived to regret it. Early in his career as a dealer he bought a magnificent secretary that he was sure would sell right away. It was truly beautiful and the most imposing he had ever seen. That was the trouble though. Counting the lovely carved "bonnet" at the top, the secretary stood a full 9 feet tall. Most ceilings today are 8 feet high. Many customers admired the piece but it took a full eighteen months before someone came along who not only had the money to purchase such a beauty but the 10-foot ceilings to accommodate it. Fortunately this was the only "dog" (albeit a beautiful one) in his shop, because no dealer can make it with such a slow turnover of stock.

One way to survive the inevitable slow periods is to have a good supply of inexpensive antiques which will sell readily. It is usually far easier, for instance, to sell four Art Nouveau lamps at $95 each than one bookcase at $395. Many dealers, therefore, keep plenty of framed prints, small mirrors, lamps, and "collectables" on hand. Some go much further and handle a wide variety of small nonfurniture items—sterling silver souvenir spoons, china cups and saucers, dolls, crystal stemware, embroidered linens, and so forth. These can be sold for anywhere from a couple of dollars to $30 or $40, the price range many people seek when buying gifts.

You might also consider carrying a line of fine furniture polish. One dealer in my town keeps a few bottles of an excellent polish (not available in grocery stores) near the cash register. When the customer asks him, "How shall I care for my antique?" he has a ready answer. He suggests a bottle of the polish and the customer invariably buys one. The dealer makes a couple of dollars' profit on the polish and the customer is delighted to have this high quality product to care for the antique.

Some dealers also add to their profit potential, as well as add color to their shops, by selling hand-crafted, old-fashioned-looking accessories on consignment. This could include pieced and quilted pillows, needlepoint pictures, embroidered aprons and linens, or any other type of quality gift item. The dealer takes a 10 or 15 percent commission on the selling price in exchange for handling the sale. Just be careful that you don't go overboard with the artsy-craftsy things. I know of one dealer who loaded her shop down so with pot holders, quilts, stuffed dolls, and linens that customers could hardly find the antiques! She eventually went out of business even though three other antique shops on the block thrived.

This brings up another point often debated by antique dealers. Is it better to specialize in certain categories (only pre-nineteenth-century furniture, for instance) or to fill your shop with an eclectic mix of all styles, periods, prices, and categories. One side of the argument says you must specialize because you can't possibly know everything there is to know about every type of antique. This theory says you should pick one small portion of the antiques market and learn everything you can about it. You should then cater to the customers who are looking to fill out collections of *that* particular style or period.

The other side says an overall good knowledge about antiques in general is enough; you don't have to be an *expert* on everything. According to this thesis, you must have a variety of merchandise to stay in business; specialization too severely limits your profit potential.

This problem is one you'll have to resolve for yourself. Too many variables exist to make a generalization that would apply to every shop in every town. If, for instance, yours happens to be the only antique shop in town I think you'd be foolish not to carry a variety of merchandise. You'd be cutting yourself out of too much business otherwise. On the other hand, you may live in a town where every other shop stocks a mixture of all styles and periods, and yet there is a heavy demand for fine antiques made before 1830. You would be doing yourself a distinct favor then to learn all you could about furniture made before the age of machinery, and then stock your shop with *only* those very old, expensive, and desirable antiques. You'd find a ready market among those customers who would come to you regularly because they would have confidence in your expertise and your merchandise.

As happens with every retailer, you'll undoubtedly find yourself occasionally with a few pieces that just won't move. You have to make a decision then. If you think the antique is really a good, salable item then take it out of stock for a few months. When reintroduced to the sales floor later the antique will be new to many of your customers and probably forgotten by those who did see it at one time. Its chances of selling are revived. On the other hand, if you find yourself stuck with an obvious mistake, reduce the price drastically and get it out of the store. Better to take a loss than to have customers become bored with looking at the same old merchandise.

PRICING AND BARGAINING

One of the most satisfying aspects of the antiques business is that you have absolute control over your prices. No manufacturer can advertise a set price, and "fair trade" doesn't exist in this business. Also, each antique is unique, so your competition is unlikely to have an identical piece. You only have to be concerned with offering your customers good merchandise at a reasonable price, not the *same* price as other dealers.

This flexibility, coupled with your ability to buy antiques at low prices and refinish them yourself, gives you an opportunity to make some money. You'll discover, as you become knowledgeable about what and where to buy, that the profit potential in this business is as high or higher than any other legitimate business around today. Where some high-volume stores delight in making 10 to 15 percent profit after expenses, yours can easily be many times that figure. Many antique dealers regularly mark up their stock 200 or 300 percent over cost. As a refinisher and dealer you may be able to top even that ratio.

When setting your prices don't just take into consideration your cost for the antique and the refinishing materials used on it. You must consider the rent on your building, insurance on your stock, utilities, advertising, salaries (if you hire help), and a small margin to allow for markdowns. Too, you had to spend some of your time and gasoline to ferret out those antiques in the first place. Don't forget your acumen in finding the antiques and your skill in refinishing. These are worth something too. A doctor or lawyer charges heavily for years spent learning the profession. You're entitled to the same consideration. Add up all these factors and *then* tack on your profit.

You may have to allow for delivering some large items, too. Many shops will deliver any antique without charge to any address within the city limits. I know of one dealer who will deliver an antique *anywhere* a truck can go, but he charges fifteen cents a mile, one way, on all deliveries outside the city limits.

Should you set firm prices or be willing to negotiate? Some shop owners do not like to haggle over prices. To them it is undignified and unbusinesslike. They prefer to set what they consider a fair price and stick with it. Other dealers, knowing how many collectors delight in bargaining, routinely price their antiques about 10 percent above the figure they're willing to settle for. After a little polite and good-natured bargaining, they cheerfully drop the price, the customer says, "I'll take it," and leaves feeling he or she made a good deal. This is a good selling technique. Most customers cannot resist buying an antique they genuinely want if they can get it for less than the marked price.

Dealers almost universally give one another a 10 percent discount on antiques. And since it is assumed the antique is for resale, no sales tax is charged. Just be sure to note the dealer's sales tax number on the sales slip for your own records. Your local tax department may require this information when you file your returns at the end of the year.

Whether discounting to customers or other dealers, make a shop policy on just how much you will lower any one item. Then stick with that decision! Better to miss a sale once in a while than to sell a good piece at such a low price you make no profit on it.

MERCHANDISING TECHNIQUES

You will probably want to be a step ahead of your competition in some way, especially when you first open your shop. Perhaps you can stay open until 5:30 p.m. when every other shop closes at 5:00. Customers who are shepherded out of every other shop on the block at closing time will often gravitate to the one that is still open. And interestingly enough, these last few minutes of the sales day are often when many shops make the fastest sales. People have finished "looking" and are ready to buy, so the shop that's still open is the one most likely to make the sales.

Maybe you can devise some type of sales incentive that will make buying at your shop a little more attractive than at other shops. I know of one dealer who gives a small bag of potpourri with each purchase. (She makes it herself and it costs very little.) Another signed up with the local welcome service and offers a 10 percent discount on every new customer's first purchase. You might price your antiques just a bit lower than the competition for the first few months until you develop a following.

One good selling technique used by almost every successful antique shop is a file of customer "wants." All this takes is a card file box and a supply of 3 in. × 5 in. cards. Whenever someone asks for an item you don't have in stock, you just note the item and the person's name, address, and phone number on a card. File the card under the item, and then when you get one in you call the customer or drop him or her a note. Most people appreciate this personal touch and you will make many sales that otherwise would be lost.

You will almost surely have to have some sort of layaway plan. Be prepared with a rubber stamp which details the terms of the agreement, and then imprint this stamp on the face of the sales receipt. The stamp should state the number of days the item will be held. Most stores allow ninety days for an item to be paid off and picked up. Ask for a 25 or 30 percent down payment and the balance in weekly or monthly installments.

Sometimes a purchase will have to remain in the store for days, weeks, or even months after the sale until the buyer has a place for it or until it is paid for. If you're crowded for space and have antiques waiting to be brought out onto the sales floor you'll probably want to move the sold piece into the store room or closet. However, if you have the space to spare, you can subtly advertise the fact that your antiques sell well by using the ploy of a friend of mine. She had some distinctive red cards printed which announce in bold black letters, "*Sold!*" She places one of these on every antique which is sold but waiting for pickup or delivery. The cumulative effect of a few of these cards on a customer is undeniably, "This is a successful shop where sales happen fast. If I see something here I want I'd better buy it because it may not be here long."

A useful, attractive, and reasonably priced antique will sometimes sell itself, especially if the customer makes several return visits to the store to examine it. You'll make many more sales, however, and more often on the customer's first visit, if you use some of the proven techniques of selling these luxury items. (And antiques, like diamonds, *are* considered luxuries, even though, again like diamonds, they also are considered excellent investments.)

I've found three methods to be particularly useful when showing an antique to a customer. First, demonstrate the beauty of the wood's patina and the sturdiness of the construction. Explain that the craftsmen who made furniture years ago took a great deal of pride in their work. Each piece was lovingly manufactured and finished with an eye to lasting through many generations. Such is not the case with most modern furniture.

Second, explain the investment potential of an antique. For the past few years, antiques have increased in value at about 20 percent a year. Barring a major depression, experts see no reason for this trend not to continue. At the same time, a piece of modern furniture, regardless of its original value, can lose up to 80 percent of the selling price as soon as it leaves the store. It immediately becomes just used furniture.

Third, try to find some interesting tidbit of information you can give the customer about the particular antique under consideration. You might tell something about the people who lived and used that style and why it was popular at a particular period. This is where a good background in the history of antique furniture can be invaluable. I had a pretty little mahogany table once which usually attracted only casual attention. It was only when I told some customers that the table was a lady's writing desk circa 1865 that they became really entranced with the graceful lines and color of the wood. Suddenly they could visualize a hoop-skirted belle sitting there as she penned letters to a beau at some far-off military post. Because of my little anecdote the table developed a personality of its own. Before that it was just a table.

However, don't hover over your customers with a constant stream of chatter. Many people like to inspect an antique, go away, think about it for a while, and then come back to buy. You can irritate and alienate customers by being *too* enthusiastic with your sales pitch.

Once your shop is in operation you can increase your sales volume immensely by forming an alliance with the interior decorators in your town. Decorators often have a free hand in decorating the homes and offices of well-to-do clients and they usually don't quibble about prices. You'll find working with them an excellent way to place your most expensive pieces. You might invite all the decorators in town to a festive wine-and-cheese "after hours" party at the shop. This would give you a chance to demonstrate your antiques in a relaxed, social atmosphere.

Running an antique shop successfully means you must be a good businessperson, of course. You should have a flair for merchandising, know how to promote your business, and be able to get along with customers. However, even more important than those factors, according to many studies, is that you have a thorough knowledge of antiques. If you know and love antiques and can discuss them with enthusiasm, your customers will feel confidence in you as a dealer.

Increase a customer's knowledge of antiques by cheerfully sharing your own and you'll make friends with everyone. They'll come back to you as a dealer because they'll have confidence in your expertise and because they, too, want to become more knowledgeable about antiques.

Many, many antique dealers had absolutely no prior experience at retailing before they opened their own shops. But the vast majority of those antique shops are successes today, mainly because practically no one goes into this business unless he or she really loves antiques. Add some basic knowledge to this love, plus good merchandising, and you have a winning combination that's hard to beat!

OTHER WAYS TO MAKE MONEY WITH YOUR ANTIQUES

You may become seriously involved in restoring antiques and want to start making a profit on your "hobby," an avocation more accurately described by long-time buffs as an "obsession" and "disease." Yet you do not have the desire or time to manage an antique shop full-time. Several other options are open to you.

SELLING ON CONSIGNMENT

One answer is to sell on consignment through other people's shops. Hundreds of antique dealers sell their wares this way and it could well be the most satisfactory method for you, too.

Consignment selling is quite simple. In return for certain services, you give the shop owner a commission of a certain percentage on each sale. This percentage varies from community to community but averages between 15 and 30 percent of the sales prices. As with most other exchanges in life, however, this percentage is often negotiable.

I've placed my antiques in several shops in the past few years at several quite different commission rates. The terms depended upon the services I received and the shop owner's enthusiasm about having my merchandise in the store. Sometimes, if you find just the right situation you can pay a commission as low as 10 percent. This has happened to me twice. About the only way you can work out such a deal, however, is when antiques are not the shop's main source of revenue. Many merchants today realize that a few antiques add a touch of elegance to their places, in addition to being excellent for displaying merchandise. One very pleasant consignment arrangement was with the owner of a small gift shop. She dealt primarily in handmade items. She had hundreds of charming stuffed animals, pot holders, quilts, wood carvings, wall plaques, and door decorations. Each item in her shop was on consignment from one of dozens of creative men and women. The shop owner had nice merchandise but rather poor display methods. So I approached her with the idea of putting a couple of small tables and a few chairs in the shop. She was delighted with the idea since her merchandise would be far more attractive when displayed on my antiques. The understanding was that each of my antiques would be plainly marked with a sales price.

This worked out quite well, since her license specifically covered consignment merchandise. So we had no legal or contractual problems in her selling my antiques. She just sent me a check, minus her 10 percent commission, each month to cover sales. She collected the tax and included it with her own reports.

The other deal was a little different. It was with a prestige men's clothing shop. The store is quite unique, tastefully decorated in a Victorian motif with stained-glass chandeliers, thick carpets, and classical music on the overhead public address system. The owner was quite interested in putting some of my antiques in the shop, not only for display purposes but also to help carry out the old-fashioned theme. Now, his business license did not cover consignment selling, so he could not handle sales for me. This turned out to be no real problem, though. Whenever a customer showed interest in one of my antiques the shop owner just gave him one of my business cards and asked him to get in touch with me personally. The customer and I worked out the sales arrangements between the two of us. The shop owner never handled any money or collected any taxes for me. But I did give him a 10 percent "finder's fee" on each sale from his shop.

Most antique consignment deals, however, are with the owners of antique shops. And on the whole, this is where you'll have the best luck with consignment selling. Disadvantages as well as advantages do exist, of course, with consignment selling, and you should understand them before going into any such arrangement with another dealer.

Some of the advantages are:

1. You gain excellent and continuous exposure for your antiques in the ideal showcase—a shop where people come specifically to browse and/or buy antiques.
2. Shop owners who have the space usually are quite happy to work with you as a consignor, since they risk none of their own capital and yet have an opportunity to make a profit on your antiques.
3. You don't have to manage a shop and deal with customers. Someone else handles sales and gets the merchandise out the door.
4. You usually develop a close friendship with the store owner. This is valuable in helping you learn more about the business of buying and selling antiques.

Some disadvantages of consignment selling are:

1. You must pay the consignee a substantial commission for displaying and selling your antiques.
2. You can't control all circumstances regarding your antiques while they are in the shop (theft, fire, damage), since they are not in your physical possession.
3. You can't control the way your antiques are displayed. Many retailers give the best selling spots to their own merchandise rather than to consignment items.
4. Any retailer, given a choice between pushing his or her own merchandise or yours to a customer, will quite naturally choose the former.

Your relationship with the store owner is what is termed an "agency relationship." This means he or she never takes title to the merchandise but acts only as your agent in passing title to the buyer. Therefore, since the consignee never *owns* the merchandise, any liability for loss remains with you. You may be able to make an agreement with a consignee to share any loss, but in the absence of such an agreement, you are responsible for any loss involved.

You need to be aware of other legal implications of consignment selling. First, you should have a contract with the consignee which stipulates exactly what the terms of the agreement might be. This can be a quite simple document as long as you spell out all the facets of the relationship. The terms should include such items as: which of you picks up and delivers the antiques to the shop, the amount of the commission the consignor pays the consignee, and the length of time the consignee will keep the antiques in the shop. You should specify which of you has the final say on pricing, and that no price (once decided upon) will be reduced without your knowledge. You should have a clear statement of how and when payment will be made to you for those antiques that sell.

By and large, the following is an accurate statement of the status of a consignment agreement, based on many court decisions:

1. The consignor may demand return of the merchandise at any time.
2. The title rests with the consignor until the merchandise is sold. At that point, the title moves directly to the buyer and never passes through the consignee.
3. The consignee may return unsold goods at will and without obligation.
4. The consignee is authorized to sell the goods only at the specified price or not less than the agreed-upon price.
5. The consignee must forward proceeds of any sale immediately to the consignor or deposit them in a special account.

Don't be frightened away from consignment selling by all this legal talk. If you have any doubts, consult your attorney. Thousands of antiques are sold this way every year, quite to the satisfaction of everyone involved.

SELLING FROM YOUR HOME

Another way you can run a part-time antiques business is by selling from your home. The nice thing about this way of dealing is that you have absolute control over the date, time, location, and items involved in the sale.

You can sell one or two antiques at a time if you like. Look in the classified section of your daily newspaper under the "Antiques" listing. You'll probably see a few ads offering buffets, tables, dressers, or whatever. Some of these ads, of course, were placed by people who simply want to sell the antique because they have no use for it. A few, however, will probably be placed by people who sell antiques regularly as a part-time business. They find this method of advertising to be highly effective and quite economical.

I'll pass along a little hint about writing those ads in case you should decide to try this type of selling. You will increase your ratio of sales if you have *several* of the same type of item to sell each time you run an ad. But you actually only list *one* of them. For instance, your ad might read:

> Antique rocking chair, completely refinished, excellent condition. $175. 555-8233.

Now, you might actually have three rocking chairs of different descriptions and selling for different prices. So when the phone calls start coming in you just describe all *three* rocking chairs to each caller. The chances are at least one of your descriptions will intrigue each caller and he or she will be interested enough to come by your home. When the first rocker sells you just describe the two remaining rockers to the next callers. When another sells, you describe the third and last rocker to the callers. You could, of course, describe all three rocking chairs in the ad but that would make it quite long and expensive. This little trick can save you many dollars in advertising costs.

If you have several different types of antiques to sell at one time you should list each one. You might run an ad that says:

> ANTIQUES for sale! Oak princess dresser, $195; mahogany dining table, $650; walnut Victorian bed, $350; matching commode, $225. All completely refinished. 555-6655.

Don't use such terms as "much more" to indicate additional items. Most people who are looking for a specific piece of furniture will not respond to an ad unless that item is listed.

The big disadvantage of selling one or a few antiques at a time is that you tie yourself to your phone and home for the run of the ad. If your ad runs for a week then you should be at home most of the time that week to answer phone queries and direct people to your home. You'll be answering the phone many, many times and showing the antiques at all hours of the day and night.

An easier and more effective way to sell from your home is to have one big sale a year. Set aside one Saturday and plan to do nothing else that day except show and sell your antiques. You save your time and you'll draw a large crowd of buyers who may come for one item but actually end up buying more.

An ad for this type of sale might read:

BIG ANTIQUE SALE!

Library table, marble-topped lamp table, set of four chairs, odd side chairs, rocking chairs, fern stand, fainting couch, pine commode, dressers, china cabinet, floor lamps, frames, mirrors.
Saturday, June 14, 8:00 a.m. to 4:00 p.m.
123 McKinley Drive

I guarantee such an ad will draw a crowd! Notice that you don't list your phone number in this ad. You don't want to spend time on the phone describing all those pieces of furniture. And you don't want to give people a chance to wheedle you into showing them at another time than that stated for your sale day.

One word of caution about such a sale. You should check local zoning laws to make sure such a sale is legal in your neighborhood. This is really not a garage sale and you might be bending some regulations about in-home businesses. In any event, I would advise you to charge sales tax on every sale *if* you have applied for and received a license as a legitimate dealer. Most communities regard any sale made by a dealer to be taxable whether that sale is made in a shop, in a home, at a show, or wherever.

GENERAL HINTS ON ADVERTISING Regardless of the kind of sale you plan, you should know a few basic rules of effective newspaper advertising. Follow these guidelines and you can hardly go wrong:

    1. Catch the reader's attention in some way. Often this will be by having the word "antiques" in upper-case letters as the

first word in the ad. Use large-size type and don't crowd it. White space may cost you more money but it is a good way to make your ad stand out in those long columns of closely set type. If your newspaper offers such a service, you might set your ad off with a star or check mark. These are good attention getters.

2. Include the price of each item if that is practical. Most readers like to know the price of something before they inquire about it. You won't be able to do this if you have a long list of antiques which includes several similar items with different prices.

3. Use simple words and short sentences. Don't use meaningless phrases such as "priced to sell." Why else would you be running the ad if you hadn't priced the things to sell? Make every word a selling word. Use descriptive adjectives so people will be intrigued about the item. "Curved-glass oak bookcase secretary with beveled mirror" would be better than "oak secretary," for instance.

4. Avoid abbreviations. Make it easy for readers to understand and respond to your ad. Don't make them wade through underbrush such as "rosewd. Q.Anne din. tabl., 6 chrs., perf. cond."

5. Run the ad long enough for it to be seen by a large number of people. Not everyone reads the paper every day. It's usually less expensive day for day to contract for a seven-day rate than for three days, for instance. You can always cancel the ad if the item sells the first day or so, then get a refund on the unused time.

6. If your paper has a "bargain box" section in the classified pages be sure to use it. This section, which lists only items under a certain price, is often the first read by many people. My local paper, for instance, lists items for $100 and less in this section. The fee for listing an item in this section is very low. I use this section whenever I have something I can sell for a low price and still make a profit.

7. Take advantage of the expertise of the ad writers at the paper. They're trained to write selling ads and can help you word yours for the best effect.

LEASING

Probably one of the least well known ways of making money with antiques is by leasing them to businesses. Yet, dollar for dollar, you can hardly beat it for making a profit.

Have you ever attended a model home or office showing where the rooms were beautifully decorated, sometimes with fine antiques? The chances are those antiques were leased from some enterprising dealer. The developer of the project, who has no use for the furniture after the promotion is over, finds it cheaper to lease than to buy. This opens a small but highly profitable market for antique dealers. It is a good deal for you, the dealer, because you collect a fee from the developer for using your antiques, then you get them back at the end of the promotion.

I once furnished an entire office in a new building with lovely old late-nineteenth-century office furniture. The realtor in charge of leasing the offices wanted to show how their starkness could be relieved with good decorating. So he hired a professional interior decorator and turned her loose with a substantial expense account. She, in turn, hired me to furnish the rooms.

I had a pretty good stock of office furniture (file cabinets, desks, swivel chairs, etc.) but not quite enough to fill those cavernous spaces. So I improvised. I used a round oak dining table with a set of four matching chairs for the conference room. A library table worked fine as a credenza. A couple of "Bible" tables served as display tables. The pièce de résistance was a one-of-a-kind high-backed triple-press swivel desk chair, circa 1865.

The decorator added paintings on the wall, plants, and warm rugs. The effect was quite charming and the realtor was delighted.

Another time I leased just one piece of furniture—a unique single Eastlake-style bed—to a fine fabric shop. The owner was having a one-month promotion to show customers the many ways fine fabrics could be used in home decorating. Part of the promotion included instructions in quilt making. She wanted my bed to show how exquisite a lovely quilt could be when displayed on an antique bed.

How do you find these opportunities to lease your antiques?

First, make friends with every good interior decorator in town. Ask them to come by your place and see your antiques and let them know you have an ever-changing stock. Get to know the developers who will be putting up new office buildings and housing developments. Let them know you are a professional who can help them sell or lease their buildings. You'll need business cards and perhaps a simple flyer with some information about yourself and your inventory.

You will need a contract to spell out the responsibilities and obligations of everyone concerned in such a deal. I've worked out the following one. It seems to cover every contingency I've ever run across.

LEASE AGREEMENT

Jacquelyn Peake, Antiques Unlimited, 201 South Grant Street, Fort Collins, Colorado (the lessor), agrees to allow _____
_____(the lessee)
to use the following antique furniture for display purposes for a period of _____
_____ beginning _____ at a fee of _____ of the
retail value of the furniture per _____ .
This agreement is renewable upon mutual consent of both parties.
In the event of theft, fire, loss, or damage the lessee _____

agrees to pay the full retail value of the furniture minus any leasing fee previously paid. A delivery fee of $_____ in addition to the leasing fee, covers both delivery of the furniture and its removal from the site.
Special terms of this agreement are: _____

ANTIQUES COVERED UNDER THIS AGREEMENT:

CODE NUMBER	DESCRIPTION	RETAIL VALUE

Jacquelyn Peake   DATE

                                                                    DATE

The fee you would charge a client for using your furniture depends entirely upon your own community. I charge 5 percent of the value of the furniture per month. I've heard of other dealers who charge 8 percent of the value of the furniture per three-month periods for long-term leases. The delivery fee is just whatever it will cost me to deliver and pick up the antiques. This has to include the truck, mileage, and rental of any equipment such as furniture dollies.

Other than the obvious profit in this type of business, I've discovered a few other angles. I always place a gold foil sticker bearing my name and address on each piece of furniture I lease out. This is constant advertising at no cost to me. And once in a while a leasee will fall in love with one of my antiques and end up buying it!

One of the biggest disadvantages of leasing furniture is having to move it in and out of the leasee's place of business. You need a truck and some muscles. A furniture dolly and pads are pretty necessary, too. All these (even the muscles) can be rented if you don't own them.

The other obvious disadvantage is that you must have a considerable amount of storage space to house your antiques between bookings. A garage will suffice, of course, if you can evict the family car.

SELLING AT ANTIQUE SHOWS

I don't know of any way to expose your antiques to more people in less time with less effort than by "working the shows," as it is known in the trade. If you've never attended an antique show, be sure to go to the next one in your area. You'll be amazed at the amount of buying and selling going on. Instead of waiting for the customers to come to them, the dealers at these shows have, essentially, gone to where the buyers congregate. These buyers come looking for good merchandise and they're willing to pay a reasonable price for their purchases.

The beauty of this type of selling is that an antique show attracts so *many* of those buyers. Literally thousands of potential customers walk the aisles of most shows—collectors, dealers, and casual buyers. For this reason, I really believe that renting a booth at a good antique show can return more profit per hour than any other form of selling antiques. To make this profit, however, you must have a good stock of those antiques which are most in demand.

As with selling from the home, selling at a show also allows control over your time. While some of the larger shows may go on for a solid week or two, most smaller ones are held on weekends. So the part-time antique dealer can easily work the schedule around other commitments. Most part-time antique dealers work one or two shows a year in their own towns, in contrast to the full-time dealers who set up a circuit that may include twenty or more shows across the country a year.

How do you get involved in working the shows? Start by attending every one within reasonable driving distance of your home. You'll find they come in all sizes. Some of the smaller ones may have space for only twenty to thirty exhibitors, while the real "biggies" in cities such as New York, San Francisco, Denver, and Philadelphia may attract hundreds of dealers.

Each show will be staged by a promoter of one kind or another. Frequently, the promoter will be a nonprofit organization such as a church or service club. These people are raising operating capital for their organizations through booth rental and entrance fees. Other shows will be organized by regular professional promoters who also work the show circuit, holding shows in many cities across the nation. They, of course, are in business, and all the profit after expenses goes to them. The professionals may sometimes have a bit of an edge over the nonprofit folks when it comes to sophistication, but that isn't always the case. Enthusiasm for their cause can make real go-getters of the volunteers when it comes to putting on a good show. One of the best every year in my town is put on by the local symphony guild.

Each promoter will arrange for preshow publicity in the media. This is vitally important, since it is the only way most buyers know about the show. So, judge for yourself the effectiveness of that publicity. Are press releases in the local paper backed up with spots on radio? Did the promoter put flyers in each antique shop in town and any other likely spots that would attract the attention of antique buyers? Is there a large, attention-getting banner outside the hall where the show is held? These are the types of things that will bring eager buyers to the show and money into your pocket.

At each show you should wander around and get a feeling for the general success of the affair. Is the building large enough to hold the dealers' booths and still allow plenty of room for customers to walk around with ease? Is the room well lit? What about the parking facilities for customers? Is some sort of food and drink available for customers? A good promoter looks to all aspects of the show, not just to getting the dealers in.

Then make another round of the room or rooms and look at the antiques on display. How do they stack up for quality? Would you be proud to show your things alongside the ones in the show? Is every booth filled? Empty booths might indicate poor management on the part of the promoter.

Talk with the dealers. Explain that you're thinking of signing up for the next show. Ask if they're happy with the show's promotion and management. Are they selling enough to justify the trouble and cost of entering the show? Ask if they've shown in that particular show before. People don't rent space a second time in a poorly run or unproductive show.

You might think the dealers would tell you to buzz off and mind your own business after such personal questions. Not very likely. Antique lovers, and all antique dealers are, like nothing better than to talk about their obsession. To them every acquisition is a conquest and every sale a way of sharing the beauty of their wares. They'll gladly talk with you and advise you about their successes and failures.

If you like all you see and hear at a show, then scout around until you find the promoter. Explain that you're a new dealer and would like to rent space in the next show. You might be surprised to hear that all booths are rented in advance for the next *two years.* That was the answer a friend and I received to our first attempt to get into a particularly prestigious local antique show. Frankly, we had no idea there was that much competition for space.

We didn't have any trouble getting into the next scheduled show, put on by another promoter, though, and we're now regulars on his list. This led to being asked to rent space in a new show in a nearby town. We now sell our antiques at both these annual shows, one in the spring and another in the fall.

The procedure for renting space in an antique show is pretty much the same everywhere. Once you decide upon the show you like, and assuming the space is available, you will be asked to sign a contract. This contract will state the place, time, and date of the next show. It will spell out the promoter's obligations as to advertising, promotion, facilities, etc. It will probably have a blank line where you fill in the type of antiques you will be bringing to the show. And it will list the price you will be charged for booth rental. This could be anywhere from $75 for a small show to several hundreds of dollars for one of the glittering events in a major city. You will probably be expected to pay half the rental fee upon signing the contract. The other half is due the first day of the show.

Let's say you've decided upon a weekend show which will run from 10:00 a.m. to 9:00 p.m. on a Saturday and from 11:00 a.m. to 5:00 p.m. on Sunday. Usually, you will be allowed to bring your antiques in on Friday afternoon and evening. The building will be locked and guarded during the nights so you don't have to worry about theft. You will set up your display on Friday evening and then arrive an hour or so early on Saturday morning to touch up.

Plan to allow some time for preopening shopping around at the other dealers' displays before the doors open to customers. You can study the other dealers' stocks and check your prices against theirs. Perhaps you'll even find the gateleg table or pier mirror you need for your own collection! Actually, an amazing amount of buying, selling, and trading goes on in that hour before the doors open. As mentioned earlier a 10 percent discount on the retail price to other dealers is customary. This is also your chance to get to know your fellow dealers and make some fine friends. They can help you understand trends and marketing of antiques at shows. So be sure to take advantage of this hour before the show actually starts.

Booth size in the average antique show probably averages about 10 ft. × 20 ft. Imagine such an area and you can see that it takes

Sharing a booth with a fellow antique dealer can be fun. Here my friend Carol and I are taking care of those last-minute pricing and polishing details in the final moments before the show opens.

quite a bit of stock to fill it. You may not have that many antiques to sell at one time. It takes quite a bit of time and capital to acquire and refinish some twenty to twenty-five major pieces of furniture. This doesn't mean you can't have the fun and profit of participating in an antique show, however. The answer is to share the space and rental fee with another dealer.

A friend and I do this for two shows a year. Neither of us deals full-time in antiques, so neither of us ever has enough stock to fill a booth but we can easily manage *half* the space. We each pay half the rental fee, which makes our up-front costs less and our profits higher. Too, she deals primarily in fine cut glass and I deal primarily in furniture, so we use my furniture to display her cut glass. This has turned out to be a beautiful arrangement for both of us. Not only does it cut our expenses and make for a full and inviting booth, but anything, including an antique show, is more fun when you share it with a friend.

I'll offer one word of advice about setting up your booth. You should always have a few real show stoppers to bring the customers in. Place one or two at the back of the booth and another at the front near the aisle. In the accompanying photograph my friend Carol and I are setting up our booth prior to a spring show. In our town good nineteenth-century oak office furniture is a hot item, so I put the file cabinet at the rear of the booth and the upholstered swivel chair at the front. The triple-press high-backed office chair was eventually moved to a center left position. I knew all three would attract attention. Sure enough, the upholstered chair sold within fifteen minutes of the show's opening and the file cabinet a couple of hours later. The high-backed chair was quite expensive and did not sell at that show. I held it over for the fall show, where it found a happy owner very quickly. All three pieces of furniture, though, brought many, many "lookers" into our booth, some of whom lingered long enough to become buyers of other items.

The only real disadvantage I see to "working the shows" is having to haul the furniture. And you have to haul back home anything that doesn't sell. Admittedly, that can be a pain. Other than that, I find shows quite profitable and just plain fun. An element of excitement, anticipation, and camaraderie exists among dealers at an antique show that is absent in other forms of selling.

I highly recommend you give it a try!

$\mathcal{G}LOSSARY$

Acanthus   A graceful leaf design used on all types of furniture, home accessories, and architectural details.

Angel-bed   An open bedstead without posts.

Apron   The flat horizontal section that separates the top of a table, desk, or chair from the legs.

Armoire   A wardrobe for hanging clothing.

Bag sewing table   A sewing table which had a fabric bag suspended below the drawer to hold work in progress. Popular during first half of the nineteenth century.

Balloon back   A favorite Victorian-style chair back, resembling an inflated balloon.

Baluster   The leg of a piece of furniture, often a central column on a table. Usually with bulbous sections alternating with smaller turned sections.

Balustrade   A series of balusters supporting a rail.

Banding   A thin strip of veneer used to decorate the top or edge of a piece of furniture; always of a different type of wood than the body of the piece.

Banister   A slender baluster.

Baroque   A fanciful, ornate style of decoration using many extravagant curves and much deep carving.

Bedstead   The frame of a bed, including posts, head- and footboards.

Bentwood   Round pieces of wood bent by steam and formed to serve as the supporting members of furniture. Often used on Victorian rocking chairs.

Bib box   A wooden box used to hold books and valuable papers.

Binder cane   The strips of cane used to edge and finish off hand caning on a chair.

Block front design   A style where the front of a case piece is formed with alternating blocks, usually the outer ones being extended and the center one recessed.

Bombe   A style often used on chests of drawers. Serpentine horizontal line, the vertical line swelling out at the bottom.

Bonnet   The upper, often elaborate, section of a cabinet or clock.

Bracket   A projecting support or ornament, used between the top of a table or other piece of furniture and its legs or base.

Brass or brazen foot   Ornamental brass casings made to enclose the ends of furniture legs.

Breakfront   A style of bookcase or sideboard where the continuity of the front surface is broken by a projecting or receding middle section.

Broken pediment   A triangular pediment with the central upper portion cut away.

Buffet   A sideboard to store linens and china and to hold serving pieces during a meal.

Bunfoot   A common foot style used on furniture primarily during the William and Mary period; shaped like a bread bun.

Bungie cord   A strong elastic cord with hooks at either end.

Bureau   Synonymous term for chest of drawers.

Cabriole leg   A furniture leg based on the cyma curve.

Cameo carving   Carving resembling delicate raised cameo cutting.

Cant   Term indicating a sloping or angled surface or edge.

Card table   A table for four, used for card playing. The top usually had narrow side leaves or a top that folded over itself. Popular from William and Mary period through Victorian period.

Carpet cutter   An early form of rocking chair where the rockers were very narrow, usually less than an inch thick. The rockers extended up into the chair's legs rather than being attached to the ends.

Cartouche   An ornament applied to case pieces, in the form of a shield or scroll.

Carver   The larger chair in a set of six dining chairs, usually with arms. Some sets had two carver chairs.

Caryatides   Figures of women, usually in classical form, used in place of columns or legs on furniture.

Case furniture   Furniture made to enclose or store items, i.e., chests, cabinets, desks, and so forth.

Casket box   A small wooden or leather box to hold jewelry and valuables.

Caster   The small wheels on the base of furniture legs. Early ones were of wood, later ones of metal or porcelain.

Caul   A strip of wood used to protect other wood from damage due to the pressure of metal clamps.

Chaise lounge   An upholstered couch, often backless, with one end resembling the back of a chair.

Chamfered corner   A corner which has been cut or planed to eliminate the sharp right angle, and in so doing forms another, wider angle.

Chest-on-chest   A tall case piece consisting of a smaller chest of drawers attached to the top of a larger chest of drawers.

Chest-on-frame   A chest of drawers or cabinet mounted upon a matching framework or desk. Made as two separate pieces.

Chest table   The lower section or frame of a chest-on-frame.

Chiffonier   A delicately designed sideboard popular during the Victorian period. Narrower than the usual sideboard, it had a shelf or two at the top and enclosed shelves below. The lower cupboard doors often had gathered silk inserts.

Circa Term meanings "about" or "around" in terms of time. Abbreviated to "c."

Classic styles Styles in emulation of the ancient Greek and Roman styles.

Claw and ball foot A carved animal or bird's claw grasping a ball, used as the terminus of a leg or post.

Claw foot A foot shaped like an animal's paw.

Commode A small, low chest of drawers.

Console A small table with three legs. The back of the table is flat to fit against a wall, the front usually being a half circle. Two legs at the back and one in the front.

Corner chair A chair with a back and one arm, designed to fit into a corner.

Court cupboard An ornate open cupboard, usually of oak, designed to store household linens and to display treasures.

Cyma The double curve in which a convex curve and a concave curve are joined as one.

Dovetail A joint formed from two interlocking wedge-shaped parts, usually used on drawer sides.

Dowel A wooden pin, usually round, used in place of nails on antique furniture.

Drop-front desk A desk with the writing surface on hinges. This surface is supported by chains while in use as a desk. When not in use the writing surface is raised, becomes a lid, and is secured with a clasp.

Escutcheon A wooden or brass ornamental plate which surrounds a keyhole.

Etagere A highly ornamented whatnot.

Field bed Bed with four high posts and a domed, framed canopy.

Finial Decorative terminal part which projects upward from the top of a case piece, lamp, clock, or frame.

Fluting Long, rounded grooves carved into wood, usually in a series of four or more.

Fretwork Ornamental wooden trim consisting of interlaced straight and curved lines.

Frieze A horizontal band of decorations.

Gesso A mixture of plaster of Paris and water used to surface and make trims for architectural and decorative articles.

Gilding Gold leaf applied to a surface, directly on wood or on a plaster of Paris decoration.

Gimp A decorative braid used to trim upholstery.

Gothic A style emulating medieval architecture, characterized by the pointed arch.

Harlequin Furniture which contains secret compartments, usually revealed by touching hidden springs.

Highboy A tall case piece consisting of a chest of drawers placed on a matching frame. The frame usually has drawers.

Hoof foot A table or chair foot in the shape of an animal hoof.

Hoosier cabinet A free standing kitchen cabinet, usually consisting of shelves behind doors in the upper section, a flat work surface, and drawers or flour bins in the lower section. Frequently, the upper section contains a flour sifter.

Incised carving   Carving where the design is cut into and below the surface.

Inlay   Pieces of wood, metal, shell, ivory, and other materials set into the surface of wood to form pictures or decorative motifs.

Knee   The projecting, curved part of a chair or table leg.

Knife box   A pierced and slotted box made to hold cutlery.

Ladder-back chair   A style characterized by a series of three or more horizontal slats set into upright side posts.

Love seat   A small couch intended to seat two people.

Lyre   A graceful design used for the ends of tables and backs of chairs, named for the musical instrument of the harp family which it resembles.

Marquetry   Decorative inlay work composed of small pieces of veneer of various woods, arranged to form a design against a background of a contrasting color wood.

Marriage   The joining of two or more major parts of as many antiques to form one piece.

Mortise and tenon   An especially strong wood joint consisting of a hole cut into one section with a related projection in the other. The two fit closely together when joined.

Ogee curve   The cyma curve constructed with the convex portion above and the concave portion below, as in the letter "s."

Ovals   The generic term used to describe the popular, plain oval frames (often with curved glass) of the nineteenth century.

Patina   A characteristic deep soft glow on wood which comes with years of use and polishing.

Pediment   A triangular or curved ornamental top for a case piece.

Pembroke table   Small breakfast table with drop leaves and, usually, X-crossed stretchers.

Piecrust-edge table   A table with three legs whose top is carved from a solid piece with a raised and fluted edge.

Pier mirror   A tall, narrow mirror, often placed above a low table.

Pier table   A low table made to stand between two long windows.

Pole bed   Bed placed lengthwise against a wall. Midway between foot and head a tall pole supports drapery which extends to the head and foot.

Quarter-sawing   A form of sawing, now outmoded, where the rings of the tree form an angle of 45/90 degrees with the wide surface of the board.

Quartetto tables   Set of four tables which nest one under the other.

Raised carving   Carving where the raised surface varies to different planes.

Relief carving   Carving where the raised design is fairly uniform in height above the surface.

Reproduction   A modern copy of an antique.

Rococo   A style of decoration, developed in France, characterized by elaborate and profuse flowing curves and motifs, often deeply carved designs imitating foliage, shells, scrolls, and so forth.

Sawbuck table   Swedish-inspired table with the top supported at either end by X-shaped members joined by a long stretcher.

Scroll feet   Furniture feet which resemble rolled up scrolls.

Secretary   A drop-front desk surmounted by a bookcase top. Also, a side-by-side arrangement with the glass-fronted bookcase alongside the desk.

Serpentine   A style usually used on dressers or chests of drawers where the front is curved, usually with two outer convex curves and one inner concave curve.

Settle   A primitive form of seat which is essentially a long chest with a lid having a high back and low arms.

Sewing rocker   A low, armless rocking chair.

Shield-back chair   Style where back fans out in oval shape.

Shim   A thin, wedge-shaped piece of wood or metal used to fill a space (n.); to fit with a shim (v.).

Skirt   The vertical band of wood on a table which is just below the top.

Slant-top desk   Similar to a drop-front desk, with the lid forming an angle when closed. Sometimes supported when open with pulls rather than chains.

Sleigh bed   A bedstead with a high headboard and footboard, each rolled outward.

Slipper chair   A low chair with short legs, used by women to change their shoes.

Splat   The flat board which extends from the top rail to the seat in chair backs.

Spline   The thin pieces of cane which hold sheet cane in chair grooves.

Split spindle   A spindle split lengthwise into two parts. Applied as ornament to case pieces.

Spoon-back chair   Style in which the back is formed to fit the contours of the human spine.

Stretcher   The horizontal members which brace and joint the legs of a piece of furniture.

Tambour   Narrow strips of wood glued and nailed to cloth. Used to close rolltop desks, Hoosier cabinets, and so forth.

Tester   The fabric covering for a framework which tops the four tall posts of a bed.

Tilt-top table   Small table or candle stand constructed so the top can be tilted up on a hinge and locked in place.

Transitional   Term used to describe any piece of furniture which transcends two or more styles and which contains elements of each.

Tripod tables   Three-legged tables whose legs slope outward from top to base.

Trundle bed   A small bed on casters which rolls underneath a regular bed when not in use.

Veneer   Thin cabinet wood used to top wood of lesser quality.

Washstand   A small table, sometimes with drawers and/or compartments, made to hold a basin and pitcher.

Windsor chair   Any of several styles of chair, all with slender spindles rising from a wooden seat.

Wire brads   Small nails of a uniform thickness, often used to attach trims and moldings.

RESOURCES

The following are a few sources of materials for refinishing antiques. Write to them for catalogs.

1. WSI Distributors
   1165 First Capitol Drive
   St. Charles, MO 63301
   (Reproduction hardware, fiber seats, caning supplies and tools, trunk hardware, finishing materials, veneers)

2. Albert Constantine & Sons, Inc.
   2050 Eastchester Road
   Bronx, NY 10461
   (Veneers, woodworking tools, finishing supplies)

3. Charlotte Ford Trunks, Ltd.
   Box 536
   Spearman, TX 79081
   (Reproduction trunk hardware and supplies)

4. Frank's Cane and Rush Supply
   16442 Gothard
   Suite D
   Huntington Beach, CA 92647
   (Caning supplies and tools)

5. The Finishing Touch
    5636 College Avenue
    Oakland, CA 94618
    (Fiber and leather seats, caning supplies)

6. T.I.E.
    P.O. Box 1121
    San Mateo, CA 94403
    (Caning supplies and tools)

7. Professional Product Research, Inc.
    65 19th Street
    Brooklyn, NY 11232
    (Pumice sanding blocks)

INDEX